From DOA

to a

New Purpose...

"This Book"

Momma Doris, Thanks for all the clean lessons! I love you.

Kathy Mendenhall

Kathy Mendenhall

ISBN 978-1-64349-559-0 (paperback)
ISBN 978-1-64349-560-6 (digital)

Christian Faith Publishing, Inc.
832 Park Avenue
Meadville, PA 16335
www.christianfaithpublishing.com

Printed in the United States of America

In memory of "Meemaw"

This Book is dedicated to my mother-in-law, Analee Mendenhall, because before I ever read the word of God for myself, she was the word. Her picture should be beside the word *grace* in the dictionary because she exemplified that word and brought it to life better than anyone I have known.

Although she was in a nursing home throughout my difficulties and had no knowledge of what I was going through, I could always feel her presence and prayers every time I thought of her.

My oldest son named her Mee-Maw even though she preferred to be called Gram-Maw, and all of the older grandchildren called her by her preferred name. But Jared refused to call her that, so my family knew her as Mee-Maw. We loved her very much.

When we think about grace, it is usually associated with our Christian salvation; however, Paul argues that to be under grace involves believers conquering the power of sin in their lives through the power of the Holy Spirit. Paul is establishing an aspect of the new covenant as seen in Ezekiel 36:25–27, where he suggests that the Holy Spirit will "move you to follow my decrees and be careful to follow my laws." Mee-Maw never gratified the desires of the sinful nature but allowed her transformed life to be contagious and desirable to those who knew her. I understood grace because of who she was, and even though I tried very hard to imitate it, I couldn't even make cookies or potato salad like she did.

I will always be grateful for the loving example of a wife and mother she was to me. Thank you, Mee-Maw.

Acknowledgments

Thank you Mark and Susan Jackson for your help, wisdom, and encouragement in my writing of "This Book." Thanks to all of the funny people in my life that unwilling became characters in "this book." all of the Christians that I am privileged to call friends for all prayers, cards, visits and support, I thank you all.

As a youth pastor's wife, I had the privilege of leading and mentoring many amazing students. I was a strong Christian wife, daughter, sister, and mother of three wonderful children. I chose to stay at home and raise my own kids, allowing for much criticism since I was a college graduate, expected to work.

I was diagnosed as a type 1 diabetic in college, and I decided that it would be easier for me to maintain my health if I just gave up sugar altogether. I am a black-and-white, type A personality. One of my previous pastors referred to me as the velvet brick, and I suppose that is fitting. I had no idea at the time, but the discipline that diabetes offered my life would later help me in so many ways. Today, it still continues to remind me to see the purpose in the process.

While everyone else enjoyed dessert, I would splurge on a coffee with lots of cream and an artificial sweetener. It really didn't bother me, and soon my body adjusted to the lack of sugar, and temptation was never an issue (except when homemade ice cream or Mississippi mud cake were on the menu). My stepmom made the best mud cake ever. It was tempting, but God promises in 1 Corinthians 10:13 that He will not allow us to be tempted above what we can handle or He will provide a way of escape so that we may be able to endure it. God provided this application of scripture to life for me way before I began to study and apply God's word consciously, and I have praised Him often for my way of escape. My Nan-Naw took my disease very seriously and would warn me often that it is a killer. I got good at endurance, thanks to my diabetes and God's grace, but it never really affected my lifestyle much except my eating.

Diabetes is a serious disease, and anyone diagnosed with it must have a good endocrinologist who keeps up with the latest changes and is willing to try new types of insulin and the latest medical developments. If I could do it all again, I would have made sure that I was having my arteries tested, and I would have counted carbohydrates every meal. I would have taken the appropriate amount of fast-acting insulin to accommodate the carb intake from the very beginning and not just focus so much on just the sugar.

Diabetes is challenging, but it can be controlled. A long happy life can be led with the proper care. Taking and controlling your sugar levels is key—meaning, testing your levels at least at every meal. It was always such an inconvenience to me that I regretfully did not do it as I should have, but hopefully, after reading my story, you will make an encouraging effort in someone else's life to do better than I did, if you don't have diabetes. If you are diabetic and you are not willing to make whatever sacrifices it takes to bring that about, you are setting yourself up for heart disease, stroke, and possible amputation. It is inevitable without proper care, I know that now.

I had people in my life that used to praise me because I withheld myself from eating sugar; however, that is only a very small part of diabetes control, and it certainly wasn't enough for me. I now wish that I had educated myself more and understood that carbohydrate control and insulin along with exercise are essential to good health.

So much progress had been made in this medical field that new forms of insulin were introduced often. In fact, I have probably taken twenty different types of insulin throughout my ordeal. I never truly understood the insulin differences or why one was used instead of another. Doctors do not have all the answers either; after all, they are practicing medicine, and it takes a lot of practice before you're ready for the big game. If you have this disease, no one can ever manage it for you as well as you can for yourself, but you have to be knowledgeable and able to fight for your own life. It will pay off and be so worth it somewhere in the future.

I was always told that if I did this then at fifty, I would be thankful. The hardest thing for me about this disease was that when I was diagnosed at twenty years of age, all the dangers that were introduced were so futuristic that I couldn't even imagine myself ever being that old. Please realize that how healthy you are when you reach old age depends on everything you do right now. At fifty-six years old, I wish I had done some things differently, but God is good, and I'm still on the right side of the grass.

God allowed my family and I to suffer some difficult times due to my diabetes, beginning with my first pregnancy. I had such unmanageable sugar levels that I could not be left alone in case my sugar bottomed out. I could not get enough oxygen to my brain, making me unable to function normally.

One night, I wrecked my mothers-in-law's car on my way home because I drove through a lady's fence and headed for her house. The police arrived and suspected I was drunk. The lady who owned the house stepped in with some orange juice and asked me to drink it. She explained to the policeman that her husband was diabetic and sometimes he gets a glare over his eyes, much like mine because his sugar gets low. After drinking the orange juice and getting some oxygen to my brain, I was able to communicate and get someone to take me home.

After that incident, my mom and my sister had to take care of me because my husband worked nights and did not want me to be left alone. He would drop me off at my mother's many times on his way to work.

1

My Buddy Mike

My husband, Mike, and I met in eighth grade in a study hall class and dated throughout high school and most of college. He was my best friend, so marrying him came easy and seemed safe because even though he was not living the way God wanted him to, his family was very religious in my eyes, and his mother was a tremendous example of motherhood and grace, something I was always so curious about.

I came from a divorced home, and I wanted so badly to be assured that I would not end up in a divorce myself. This was by far the scariest thing about marriage for me, and I wasn't at all convinced that I wouldn't follow the example I had seen. I learned again that the application of endurance is necessary in so many aspects of our lives. Mike and I had already dated for such a long time that we felt like there was nothing new to learn about one another. Boy were we wrong. Marriage can put things in a whole new perspective.

He tells people that I chased him around until I finally caught him, but I saw it very differently, of course. In those first few years of marriage, all I could think about was being a mother. I felt so incomplete without a child, so we began trying. But I had three miscarriages while I awaited the baby that was going to bring everything together in my mind.

Although I struggled through my pregnancy, we were blessed to have a beautiful, healthy baby boy who is the love of our lives and the first grandchild for my parents. I loved the whole idea of being a mother and vowed to give it everything I had.

Mike worked nights, and I worked days, sometimes literally passing one another on the road, leaving our marriage in some scary trouble. Pride didn't allow me to ever talk about it, but we were near divorce, and I was horrified.

Because of a job promotion, we soon moved from Louisville to Virginia to start another chapter of our lives, probably saving our marriage.

2

That Lady in McDonald's

After painting and working in our new home, it was time for a break. I had heard that the McDonald's in the area had an indoor playground, something that was unheard of at that time, so I decided that I would take my son on a date to give us a break and get out of the house.

I did not know one person in this new town, so I didn't bother to clean up. We just went like we were, paint in my hair, work clothes, the works. At four years old, Jared was very excited to get out of this messy unpacking environment, so off we went. We walked in and saw that the place was packed. Obviously everyone in town knew about the playground. I hurried to save a table inside the play area and then got our food.

I had been very active in a church before we moved, so it was important to me to find one right away, but at this moment I was just thrilled that I could rest and talk to no one. Just then, a woman about my age approached me and asked if she and her two girls could share our table. Since there was nowhere else for them to sit, I agreed, and as soon as she sat down, she began to spill out her life story.

Betty, as I soon learned was her name, talked as if without breathing for at least an hour. She shared that she had lost her mother, and then she found Jesus. She asked me about my relationship with Christ, making me evaluate it for the first time in my life. I had taught Sunday school, took the youth to camp every year, and worked very hard to be a part of everything that my church was doing—surely I should have been able to tell this woman all about the relationship that I had with Jesus, if I truly had one.

As I struggled to answer, I realized that I had a great relationship with the church, the physical building, and the people—but nothing with the Christ who puts it all together. I would have told anyone who asked that I was a Christian because I had walked the aisle at sixteen after feeling something stirring inside me at a Billy Graham film festival at church; however, I did not read the word or really have any knowledge of how Christ wanted to work in and through my life. I had a religion but not a relationship with Christ. Everyone was going forward, so I wanted to be like everyone else, and I stepped out and followed, having no idea that this wasn't enough.

Romans 10:9–10, the explanation of salvation, was not a scripture that I was familiar with or had made application of. No one had ever asked me if I had a relationship with Christ until this lady in McDonald's. In fact, I was unaware that anyone ever did that. She went on talking and then invited me to a Bible study that she could not stop bragging about. She told me how life-changing it was. It was so obvious to me that she really loved Jesus that I questioned why I did not. I made the mistake of giving her my phone number before leaving along with excuses of why I was not going to attend the study. She really begged me to come and asked if she could give the pastor's wife my phone number. I really just wanted to get away from all of this, but I told her it was okay.

She called me the next day and several other days prior to the study. I was amazed that she kept calling leading up to the date of the Bible study, but I kept giving her my lame excuses, fearful that I didn't know enough about the Bible to seriously study it. I wasn't even familiar with the titles of the books within the Bible. I was blown away when the pastor's wife called me and said that she was calling as a favor to one of her students. (Thanks, Betty.)

It turned out that the pastor's wife, Cathy, taught the Precept course that Betty was so engaged in. She made a caring invite, and I was so attracted to it all that I decided to go. I showed up at the next class. I finished the Philippians Bible study, thinking that I now had all the answers. The Bible made sense to me for the first time. I wanted so badly for everyone I knew to take this course and learn everything the Holy Spirit had taught me.

It was so real to me, and I wanted everyone to experience it so badly that I even took on the role of the Holy Spirit, trying to convict everyone back home of making this Bible study a part of their lives. I was accused of being self-righteous at times because my delivery of wisdom was not always conveyed properly, but after studying the word, I realized that there can be no such thing as self-righteousness because righteousness can only come from God, it is His DNA, what He is, so I was no longer insulted by the insinuation. After all, God wants all of us to grow to be more like Him, so I had to use every given opportunity to show His righteousness because without Him, righteousness cannot exist.

Thankfully, Betty, the annoying lady in McDonalds, is back in my life after thirty years, and she is one of the wisest, most wonderful people I know. Precept by Kay Arthur was my first real Bible study with many to follow, and it truly changed my life. This experience later became the reason that I got trained to be a Precept facilitator. I loved teaching His word. This gave me so many answers to questions I had dealt with for years. I studied the book of James and later facilitated the course many times. Here I learned all about joy, endurance, holding my tongue, and having a true faith. I praise God for this book, written by the brother of my Savior, for He has made clear its application for me in order that I might have a faith that is real.

This Bible Study was wonderful, and I met some amazing women who contribute to my faith today through memories of their example and teaching of righteousness. I believe that in hindsight, it is simple to determine why God places each person in your life at just the right time. There are no accidents with God. He knows the past, present, and future, so trusting Him just makes sense; then we are willing to tell others about a relationship with Him.

If you have never surrendered your life to Christ, it is certainly something you need to consider, either now or you will at His return. That is one choice you won't have to worry about making because God's word says that every knee, yours and mine, shall bow. His word, the Bible is the only truth you will ever need.

3

Swift Creek Baptist Church

As we visited churches in Richmond, Virginia, and tried to start a life far away from my home state of Kentucky, I was torn because being on our own had both positives and negatives. I was forced to grow up and depend on Mike, just as God wanted. Since I no longer had any family around, we became one, the way God intended, and He began to teach us so many things, allowing us to grow so much closer to Him and to one another.

I am so thankful for this time of our lives. Great memories.

Even though some of my family mourned our move, it became obvious to me that it was exactly what we needed.

Once we began to settle into our life in Richmond, everything became easier as we got involved in this great Bible teaching church. Mike was working on Sundays at first, so I attended with Jared every Wednesday and Sunday nights as well as Bible study on Tuesday mornings. I described this church to Mike as so unusual; it was as though you could feel the Holy Spirit every time you entered the place. I found it all very strange since I did not even have a true understanding of who the Spirit was when we started there, but I knew that I wanted whatever they had; their love was contagious. When my Sunday school class began to pray that Mike would no longer work on Sundays, it wasn't long before his shift changed and he was able to join us. He agreed that we indeed needed to be a part of this marvelous ministry.

Shortly thereafter, I was smiling from the choir loft. Since I'm really not a very good singer, they allowed me to just make eye contact and smile, someone told me to mouth "watermelon rinds" while smiling, pretending to sing, and I felt great about it, thinking I had truly found my ministry. Many people would approach me and tell me how refreshing it was to see me smiling from the choir loft. Mike and I both really learned about serving others, plus our son always came home with wonderful news about what he had learned about Jesus there.

Jared and I visited another Baptist church in the area just to make sure the one we were attending was where we belonged, and as I sat alone in the sanctuary, Jared attended the preschool program. When I picked my son up from the preschool worship, I was hoping that he really liked it because it reminded me more of the ministry we had come from in Louisville. On our way home, I asked Jared how he liked this ministry, and he said, "I liked the other church better because I learned about Jesus there." From the mouths of babes, wisdom flows. I knew that God had spoken, and at last, I was listening. Sunday school at that church we visited was so much more about who would bring the cheese to the next taco party than application of God's word.

We returned to the church where I was doing Bible study and never visited around again. I needed Bible Study time that would teach me about impacting others and discussing how God had allowed His Word to impact me. We settled in at Swift Creek, and this was a new environment that we were so thankful for. We made some lifelong friends that God placed in our lives for very obvious reasons.

I got my life together and accepted the gift of love and life from God because of this lady at McDonald's and her church. I became aware that God truly had a plan and that He had a part for me in it all. I was in awe that the Creator of heaven and earth wanted to use me to build His Kingdom.

All of this was new to me, but I wanted to know more. God instructs us to study to show thyself approved (2 Tim. 2:15). It isn't enough to read it; we have to study and make application of what we are reading so that our lives might impact others. He promises that His word will never return void. Reading a book about the scriptures is good, but it is not studying and allowing the Holy Spirit to teach your life. When you truly study and break down the verses and research their purpose for yourself, that is when the Holy Spirit teaches you personally without someone else's opinion or interpretation interfering.

I learned to interpret God's word by observation, reading and rereading, and putting everything in context. You can learn about what the Lord is saying to you, and your heart has an opportunity to change because of what He is teaching. I was learning and changing daily, and church became my refuge as I found myself getting up early in order to get my Bible study completed each week. I praise God for each of those study times; those moments made me strong in my relationship with Him. There is certainly a reason that the Bible has been a bestseller for so many years. I learned that it was indeed a relationship and not a religion.

Mike took a Master Life course with several other men very early in the morning and after finishing this twenty-six-week course, he told me that he thought the Lord was calling him to full-time ministry. He worked for a large non-union trucking company, and we were financially comfortable, living on a golf course and having all our physical needs met. However, the more prayer we put into this decision, the more comfortable we were with the fact that it was God's perfect plan for our lives at this time. Mike wanted to pastor and shepherd a church. He was growing so much and was such a faithful man that I really believed that God was truly leading him to do this. I was completely supportive of him because I had seen what all God was doing in his life and mine, plus I had studied what Ephesians teaches about being a wife, and I was trying to live out godly submission as is taught in scripture.

I was fearful of becoming a pastor's wife; I did not fit the picture of what that looked like in my own mind. I always pictured a white-haired woman who taught preschoolers, was righteous, played the piano, and sang like an angel. I had none of these things going for me. I knew that people who knew us would be shocked that we were considering this transforming life decision. My own father told us that it was foolish, and we would be poorer than a church mouse if we went through with it. He made it very clear that he wasn't for our decision. We made the decision in spite of this, and Mike began searching for what opportunity to pursue in order to get the necessary education.

He resigned from trucking, and we returned to Louisville for Mike to attend Bible college and learn a whole new way of life. Even though I was fearful of our upcoming adventure, God was faithful to encourage me daily with scripture, and I loved the idea of giving back and feeling useful.

Someone once told me that being in the ministry was like living in a fish bowl. I learned that to be true, agreeing that it should be that way, since pastoral leadership is called to be beyond reproach (Col. 1:22). Everyone was able to look at our lives and therefore could hold us to the proper standard. Accountability is a very good thing. We never had any secrets or ever tried to hide anything in our life from the church—the good, bad, and the ugly. And there was some ugly. Our family was far from perfect, and we grew from our poor choices just like others did. It was out there for all to see. I did not know what a committed pastor's wife looked like since I did not really have an example in my life growing up, and I didn't seek a mentor because I never considered that it would ever be a necessity.

Thank God, we cannot know our own future. When I was as a college student, I dated the son of a preacher, and I feared that I might actually love this other young man too, making me have to weigh Mike against him and choose. I thought that Mike was the safer choice. Believing that this pastoring thing might be hereditary and knowing that Mike would never be in the ministry, I felt assured. No one will ever convince me that God doesn't have a great sense of humor, with the joke oftentimes being on me. He can make things quite fun, and don't we all love fun? Unlike our early role models, we took our responsibility to this verse in Colossians very seriously and tried to always be the example that Christ wanted us to be.

As we walked through the ministry life as a family, like everyone, we had our ups and downs, and of course, I thought my downs were much worse than anyone else's. Don't we all? My oldest son made some very poor choices that affected our family in seriously negative ways, but I was truly taught the value of prayer through it all. I think we all want to believe that our lives will turn out the way that we have planned, but we are not privileged to the real plan, God's plan, and it rarely lines up with our own. I began to learn this lesson through many of my son's choices. My husband was faithful to hold out for the Prodigal Son (Luke 15), but truthfully, I doubted yet prayed he would be right.

I had to learn a lot about grace during these years, and I fell short often of being all that God wanted for me, but I learned to trust Him each step of the way. We prayed often as a family and encouraged one another to seek wisdom from above. I know that Mike always encouraged young men who were thinking about ministry that if they could live with themselves doing anything else besides ministry, then they should do it. He believed so strongly that it took everything you had, plus some, to commit to serving the Lord full time because it meant you would always be serving others, and it was difficult. People, even God-fearing Christians, can be very hard to work with. Mike and I served faithfully but learned that the hard way, offering us a severe lesson on the value of forgiveness.

When Mike pastored several small ministries, usually closer to our home in Louisville, it always amazed me when we would visit the membership and they would invite us into their homes; they would try to hide from us the parts of their lives they were not proud of. For instance, if someone opened the refrigerator and they had beer in it, a scene to hide the beer from us would quickly take place, only displaying an obvious conviction regarding the fact that they drank. Even though we personally chose not to, we did not dictate that others had to have our same convictions, except in our own home. It was wonderful having family closer so I could get more times to visit with them, and I knew how important it was that my son had the opportunity to know and love family. I was grateful.

4

What? Twins?

I began to be very sick every day, and I could not come up with a reasonable explanation. Mike was worried about me but felt led to re-read Genesis before bedtime. I was tired because of feeling so sick all the time so I went to bed. Finally, in a deep sleep one night, I was awakened by a very excited Mike, who said, "I know why you're so sick. You have two nations at war in your womb."

I thought he was absolutely crazy and rolled over to go back to sleep. He explained that he was reading Genesis 25 from verse 21 to the end of the chapter, where Rebecca was having twins. He insisted at four o'clock in the morning that I was having twins, and this was the reason for the sickness. I was tired and slightly annoyed that Mike thought he was now a prophet, so finally I went back to sleep as he was off to work. I had already taken a pregnancy test and ruled that out, plus I was never sick with my first pregnancy. So I gave little thought to Mike's prophecy.

I had to have a high-risk OB because of my diabetes, so I made an appointment the next day to get this all figured out, mostly to prove Mike wrong. I kept my appointment in two weeks, and after telling him how sick I was, he suggested a vaginal ultrasound. I had no idea what that entailed, but as I lay down on my back, he stuck a measuring tool into my private parts and talked to me to keep me relaxed as he measured.

He finally said, "You are certainly pregnant, and the measurement puts you at about four weeks." I was shocked that my home pregnancy test was inaccurate. But I was even more astonished when, as he was pulling it out, he said, "Wow, there's another one." I sat up, fearful, thinking, *Another what?* "Am I having a two-headed baby or what?"

He answered with, "No, another baby, silly."

My immediate response was, "Two nations at war in my womb?"

He was a Jewish man and familiar with that particular scripture, so he jokingly said that he did not often use that terminology but yes.

I was having twins. I quickly dressed and ran to the outer office to call Mike and confirm that he indeed was a prophet. The entire office knew that I was having twins by the time I was done talking to Mike. I was so thrilled, and Mike was elated on the other end of the phone to learn that I was pregnant with twins. I believe he said, "I told you so."

I couldn't wait to get home and call all my family. We did not have twins in our family, and I had no idea what we were in for. But it sounded so great that we could each have our own little one; I remembered that I hated having to share Jared with Mike at times. It seemed like he always wanted to hold and love on him when I did as well. This seemed like a perfect solution.

My mother-in-law came to stay with me as the due date got closer. As Mike's birthday approached, we went to the mall to purchase his present. I parked at one far end, thinking that it was the closest to where we were going, but it turned out that we had to walk to the other end of the mall. I have never been good with direction. I had to sit when we got there due to my elephant-leg-looking feet. Mee-Maw was worried about so much swelling, but Jared thought it was very funny for me to have such fat feet. I remember him being amazed by the fact that he could poke his little fingers into my ankle, and the imprint would stay long after he removed them.

Having twins added more high risk to the pregnancy, and my doctor told me that diabetics rarely carry twins to full term and they are often very small. I assured him that mine would be fine, and I would indeed carry to term. I took this pregnancy quite seriously, eating tofu and a lot of broccoli because I heard that they were high in vitamins that would strengthen the fetuses. I decided that I would attempt to breastfeed knowing that it would be healthier for them no matter how difficult. I shared my faith with my doctor, so I convinced him that God had this all under control so we were going to be fine. I convinced us both that I could have these babies naturally. I continued to throw up for three more weeks after.

I was new in my faith during this pregnancy, but I had a devoted friend, Cindy, who gave me a book called *From Prison to Praise* and encouraged me to praise the Lord even while puking. I really wanted to hate her at times, but she forever encouraged me with God's word and continues to teach me to be content in my circumstances no matter how difficult they become. If only I had truly learned that lesson then. God always gives us another chance to learn the important stuff. I was being given another chance to be content in the face of bad circumstances for sure.

God allowed Cindy to be very special in my life, even to this day, and I wish I were more like her. She became very necessary during my pregnancy because she lived close and stopped in to check on me often, since Mike traveled with his job. My sugars were so hard to control that one day, I was feeling very sleepy; I remember sitting on my couch and surprisingly awoke to find Cindy and her husband sitting on either side of me, very closely in order to hold me upright. Since Cindy was a nurse, she easily recognized my low sugars and immediately tried to get sugar into my system, which I usually fought. My sugar came back to a normal range, and they were able to return home. They introduced me to the meaning of close friendships, allowing me to recognize that same opportunity in many others in my future.

I had the twins five weeks early, and much like the Bible described, my daughter popped out hairy, but her brother was not holding her heel as the scripture described. My son fled upward as far as he could go and ended up transverse. I think he was hiding in my rib cage, fearful of what life would be like with a twin sister who would boss him around most of his young life.

My family was all traveling from Kentucky together in one van—my mother, father, sister, grandmother, and cousin— praying they would get there in time. They arrived outside the hospital but did not make it into the building. As I sat in that very awkward position, pushing, I could look out the now open window to see the heads of family members jumping up and down on a hill outside my window. The laughter that followed may have helped with Taylor's cooperation to come into this world and meet these crazies. Many of the staff were giggling to see my family through the window, and someone finally motioned them inside the building to truly be part of this experience.

After delivering Taylor, I thought that everyone tried to get Shane out, but he would not come. Finally after twenty-two long minutes, Dr. Petres, who had bought into my idea that God was going to take care of this and deliver them naturally, looked at me sadly and apologetically said that it had been too long and we were going to have to take him via C-section if he was going to make it. I had read about this possibly happening but denied it for myself, having my own plan and feeling assured that it was a good one. I agreed with the doctor to do whatever was best for my son, so as I held my daughter (at 6 lbs. 5 oz.) to my bosom, he cut my stomach and took Shane out; he weighed 4 lbs. 3 oz. She was obviously taking all the tofu and broccoli in the womb, so maybe he had some insight into what his life would be like.

He was taken instantly to an incubator because he was not breathing strong enough on his own. He stayed there for ten days. I had to take Taylor home without Shane but I returned to the hospital every day to feed him and hold him by placing my hands into the gloves attached to the side of an incubator box that he lived in. It broke my heart every time I saw him, and I prayed that every day they would tell me he was ready to come home.

There was a two-pound baby in that nursery as well, making me grateful for my little bird, Shane. He weighed three pounds then, and I was so afraid that I was going to break him every time I picked him up. I remember when he got home, my stepfather carried him in the palm of one hand. Shane looked like he fit there comfortably. He was so tiny that I thought he would never grow into his bodily features, but he did. I felt such a sense of pride and guilt at the same time and asked myself, "Who knew?" only to hear Shane later tell me, "God knew."

I learned so much by trial and error with the twins. At the end of the ten days, having our family complete, we set off like most young families, trying to do everything right and missing the mark more than we hit it. I often teared up while holding the twins in the football position, trying to breastfeed them. To say I had my hands full was quite an understatement. I struggled to get them on the same eating schedule, which meant little sleep for me. I quickly learned, however, that the breast pump was a great invention, allowing Mike some sleepless nights as well. We were so nervous at first that some nights, Mike and I would lie on the floor between the baby beds in their room just to assure they were breathing through the night. It was the best and the worst of times all rolled into one, and we wouldn't have changed it for the world.

Trips back to Kentucky were so loved because I wanted all my family to experience the miracles I interacted with each day. I knew that I had never seen anything cuter than the way they interacted with one another. After every visit, I was planning for the next one. I learned that living away from family certainly had its positives and negatives. Since Kentucky was a ten-hour drive, I wasn't able to go often. But one trip I remember most was with me, Jared, the twins, and our dog, Butkus, a huge Old English sheepdog. I had to pull over at a rest stop to let the dog out, leaving Jared alone with the twins in the locked car. Butkus took forever as I watched the car intently. Once Butkus ha relieved himself, we returned to the car to find everyone crying. The twins were hungry, and Jared was expressing sympathy for them and crying because he was unable to make them stop. They usually thought he was very funny, so he was not understanding why he could not bring about their laughter while making his funniest faces. That was a very long eventful trip, but we made it, and it was so worth any of the trouble.

5

Cloth Diapers

The ladies in the nursery dreaded seeing me because I only used cloth diapers. I have always been beyond frugal; some might say cheap. When the rest of the world had moved to disposable diapers for obvious reasons, I would bring a zip lock bag for them to put the dirty diapers in, and I could tell that they wished I would move to Pampers. Shane was so tiny it was difficult to get a cloth diaper folded enough to fit him. The only time that I used disposable diapers was when they first came home from the hospital. Shane came home with preemie diapers that looked much like a sanitary napkin. They had to be ordered, making it easier to decide to use cloth. This was all so new to me since Jared weighed over 8 pounds, and I could justify using disposables with him being only one child.

I did not have many friends who worked in the nursery. I think they avoided me, thinking that the opportunity to discuss the cloth diapers might present itself. No one ever told me, but I got a strong impression because oftentimes when I picked them up from the nursery, they would have on disposables. That never bothered me since my sole motivation to use cloth was strictly monetary. If only they had known, I'm sure they would have bought me some diapers, saving themselves the mess.

I remember a young girl who volunteered to babysit asking me once, "What if they pooped?" After describing how I washed them out in the toilet before putting them in the wash, she was no longer willing to babysit. The ladies in the nursery were never my best friends, but the ladies in my Bible study loved me and taught me so much. I had so many friends willing to pitch in any time I needed them. When the twins began to need baby food, I insisted on mixing my own vegetables in the blender. I wanted only the best for them, but that didn't last long since those little jars were so convenient.

Everyone says that you usually fuss more over your first child, but since there were two of them, I think I was overwhelmed and therefore overcompensated. As they grew, Taylor found her voice quickly and talked to Shane in a language all her own. She would point her finger and almost sound threatening at times as she instructed him. Shane sometimes responded with sounds but more often just smiled and continued doing whatever he wanted. Shane was much smaller but more physically coordinated than she was, probably due to the fact that he tried to get away from her all the time. She was always quick to point at him, blaming him anytime she perceived there might be trouble.

One day, while visiting a friend at Christmas, I was enjoying coffee in the kitchen while Taylor, 17 months old, made Shane get on all fours as she tried to balance standing on his back to reach something on the mantle in the other room. Hearing a huge crash, we ran to see my twins lying on the brick hearth covered in Christmas decorations from the mantle. I was terrified that someone would be hurt but saw Shane smiling and Taylor pointing at him, as usual, and knew they were all right.

Like most parents, as we reflect back, we would love to relive those days. It got easier every day that they grew and learned. We loved one another so much, and it felt like it would always be just like this. Sadly, it changes very quickly, you never get enough time to enjoy those early years. I took them out in public every chance I got, trying to show them off whenever possible. I imagined them in matching Easter outfits but was unable to find what I wanted so even though I had only made one jumper in high school home economics,

I was determined to sew them some amazing matching outfits. They did match, but that was about all you could really say about them as Taylor's dress began to fall apart before the holiday ended.

Jared, who was then five, loved being the big brother. He entertained himself often by watching *The Jungle Book*. He thought the babies were completely entertaining for a while, but he moved on quickly to other interests like *Teenage Mutant Ninja Turtles* and *The Jungle Book*. We all had *The Jungle Book* movie completely memorized by the twins first birthday. I thought we had the perfect little family, and I was challenged and proud every day as we all grew together. The "bare necessities" were what we were all about.

We still attended Bible study and church service. We never let having twins slow us down, but truth be known, if I would have had the twins first, I probably wouldn't have had any other children for fear I would have had three the next time, and that thought seemed too much.

Thanks to so many out there who invest the word of God into the lives of others, my life has truly been a testimony of the abundant return on that investment, and I am so thankful for all the opportunities.

Thank you to all of you girls who allowed me to teach and pray for you through those formidable years. It helped me so much, and I am grateful. I praise God for the Bible and understand that it is God's love letter to us, and through making application, it allows us to become more like His son Jesus. Every day we should be able to look at our own lives and see that we are not the same as we were the day before; maybe we are not where we should be, but each day, with Bible study and application, we will look more and more like Christ, defeating sin, as we get closer to His return. Thank you, Jesus.

Many times I asked God to tell me His will for my life. But it wasn't until I was teaching abstinence in the public schools in Ohio that He actually answered my prayer with scripture. 1 Thessalonians 4:3 simply spells it out for us all; it says, "This is Gods will for your life, your sanctification, and that you abstain from fornication." To be sanctified is to be set apart. It is the process of becoming more like Jesus every day as we walk this earth. The only scripture that defines God's will for us tells us that He wants our sanctification; maybe we should evaluate how closely we walk with Him and if we have enough of a case to ever be convicted or even accused of being a Christian.

6

This Book Begins

In August 18, 2013, my sugar dipped very low that night. I finally awoke weeks later in the hospital, understanding the life of a stroke patient. I had a stroke in the floor of our apartment. My husband tried to revive me through mouth-to-mouth resuscitation and CPR while our twins watched the life drain out of me.

Because of many prayers, EMS worked on me and shocked my heart on the way to the hospital. With my twins following, I was pronounced dead on arrival at the emergency room in the hospital, leaving my husband in the position of having to call my family and alert them of the situation. Other than my diabetes, I was very healthy until an open heart surgery in 2011, which I was fully rehabilitated from. The emergency room performed a tracheotomy in order to save my life; then I was put on life support. They also put a feeding tube into my stomach. I spent fifty-two days in the hospital with many doctors trying to get me better. I was hooked up to every wire, tube, and machine available. I was told that many family members visited in my early days there.

All my life, I have been a great communicator. I even majored in communication in college. But for the first time, I was unable to talk, not a sound would come out due to the tracheotomy in an effort to save me. So my stepmother, whom my dad refers to as

Google, brought me a small whiteboard so I could do more than a thumbs-up. I began to write everything down, and I got pretty good at communicating through the whiteboard. I even had multiple colors. Aside from the board, I also communicate through my emotions. I overused this a lot, so many were grateful for my white board. I cried every day and really had no explanation for it until months later when I learned it was very common in stroke patients.

My kids never witnessed me in this way, and it saddened them to see my emotions. My youngest son, Shane, who was there every moment since this all began, stayed with me and sang to me, and we watched movies until I fell asleep, which usually didn't take long. I was always thrilled to have Shane there.

7

Shane

Becoming a mother, then a Christian, surrendered to God's will, I thought I understood unconditional love, but it wasn't until this last year unfolded that I saw it so clearly. My twenty-five-year-old son has been by my side every day since this nightmare started, with my husband reminding me that he will be here until death do us part. I remember saying those words many years ago, but neither of us ever expected them to be tested in this way. I wonder how he even manages taking care of all of my responsibilities plus work every day. He has been such a trooper, plunging along yet probably in need of some psychological therapy himself. This was all way too much to take care of alone, and I believe he felt very alone in this battle.

In the past year, my son Shane has been my therapist, chauffer, doctor, cook, friend, son, and teacher; and I praise God every day that he truly displays unconditional love to me on a daily basis, making every effort to make me feel like I am never the burden that I know I am.

At twenty-four years old, a new college graduate, he had to assume a role that was truly unfair, preventing him from pursuing a career or life because he thought that he owed it to our family to step in. Shane stepped up and has literally carried me through so much suffering, reminding me often that we are holding on to hope because it's all we have.

Jared, my oldest, had been working the golf tour for six years, building and making the graphics for golf tournaments. Shane's twin sister, Taylor, had just started her career as a high school Algebra teacher the day after my stroke. I knew that I could never be as selfish as to tell my daughter how badly I wanted her to be with me. I could have never lived with myself if I had allowed those selfish desires to be made known, even though I wanted her so badly. Her school, Hunstville High, was very good to her and allowed her to be at the hospital when she could be. That had to be enough right now. She struggled with being unable to be there, but she called me often and tried her best to make me part of her new life.

Jesus was there for me but without explanation except that I was in good company because so many had suffered before me. He reminded me that Paul asked three times for the Lord to take his thorn, but God's answer to Paul, like mine, was, "My grace is sufficient." And I thank God for His grace. It has been more than sufficient, and it embarrasses me how I allowed my life to appear that it wasn't.

8

Stroke?

One day, while I was sitting alone, I began to think about a day in the life of a stroke patient, and I jotted down my thoughts about what my day consisted of.

I would sit up after a night of the trach gurgling, making me feel like I was suffocating, not allowing much sleep from the discomfort of the stroke. I would cough up a huge loogie, which I had to hold in my mouth until someone came in to give me a tissue. After mouthing the word *tissue* and *Kleenex* several times, they would finally understand and hand me a tissue box, which I wanted to guard with my life, knowing that I would need it again very soon.

A dear friend would visit, and I'd feel another cough coming. With the trach, I had little control, so as it would come out, I could only hope that the majority of my snotty mess hit the Kleenex instead of clinging to the side of her face. Next, someone on staff would enter for an X-ray, which would make me cough even more, simply because of the movement. My throat would feel like it was literally on fire, when in walked respiratory therapy, requiring I take a breathing treatment that would break it up even more, allowing more risky coughing, which was supposed to help me get it all out of there.

Because my heart was only pumping at 25 percent and the relationship between the heart and breathing is an important one, the breathing treatments were an everyday occurrence throughout my hospital stay. Part of the anxiety I felt was because so much was always going on, and due to the Lasix (a strong water pill), I had to work in a pee somewhere very soon. And I had no voice to tell anyone. I learned to write a lot of notes, and my son was happy to supply me with anything I wanted.

I started to write notes on notebooks about what was happening in my life as I tried to continue to trust that God still had a plan. The greatest relationship I had at this time was with my box of tissues; everything and everyone else was lost in the pain and uncertainty of my life. I had to be reminded about the life that I had with Christ. It did not come back to me naturally for some reason, probably because I was struggling with what had happened and how I could have no understanding of any of it. My son, nurses, and friends reminded me constantly, and thank God, all my memories came back in time, and I could depend on Him again. I could finally remember all the scripture that I had put to memory, and slowly, it was as if I was waking up from a long horrible dream.

For a long time, I felt like a prisoner in my own body because I could do nothing but watch TV and try to sleep, and I couldn't even accomplish that. I was like a Weeble except when I wobbled, I did fall down. I had no control of my left side, making every move nearly impossible. I had a great need to see improvement every day, and I was too hard on myself when I couldn't see any. Shane was there to see it and continually remind me that progress was being made. I wanted my husband to be there, but I realized very quickly that he could not because he had to work due to the costs that I was incurring daily. I had to accept the hand we were dealt with and be grateful that Shane was so willing to stay by my side.

I had a right brain stroke, causing my entire left side to no longer function. My brain was no longer connected to my nerves, not allowing for any voluntary movement. In order to ever get any comfort, it usually meant moving my left arm, leaving me in more pain than comfort. The family made fun of the moaning sound I would make any time someone would raise or even touch my arm. They eventually referred to it as my dinosaur sound, and Mike heard it the most because he was the least careful about hurting my dead arm. I was also told that I made a very ugly face when I got emotional, and Shane would laugh and point it out when he saw it was coming. Jared later referred to it as my mole face and forbade it to show up. I still did not have my full muscle strength in my face, so everything was a little crooked. I sometimes drooled out of the left side of my mouth and bit my cheek on that side often. The toothless holes in my mouth were embarrassing; therefore, I would rather keep my lips sealed. I could not smile the same at all and may never get that back, even though I have so much to smile about. Jesus has been so good to me that I have to believe Him for some new teeth and restored health.

We had so much support that I could never imagine going through this horrible experience without the Lord and the supporters He provided. I started attending a stroke patient support group, thinking I would get an opportunity to vent and finally release some of the indescribable feelings I had been harboring, but that obviously wasn't the purpose of this group because the only time we made it past the introductions, we made a decorative fruit pizza. Shane continued to take me to my group, always telling me to "play nice with the other children," making me laugh. We also kidded about going to the stroke group as if it were like AA. He would instruct me to say, "Hello, my name is Kathy Mendenhall, and I had a stroke." Shane tried very hard to make me laugh any time he could, knowing that laughter did not come as easy as it once did.

I battled with feeling so much regret and guilt because of the position I had put my son into. My husband could not be with me all the time because we had so many medical bills and he had to work so hard to maintain insurance. Shane graduated with a degree in athletic training, so he was very familiar with the treatment of many of my issues, and he truly wanted to help, not because he felt like he was the only one but because he loved me and wanted to give back. Shane became the only one I really trusted simply because he was so educated about all that I had to deal with, and he was very serious about my safety. I really needed to feel safe, and I always felt safe with him when everything inside me found itself very unsafe. I couldn't even trust that my own leg would hold me. I prayed it would not involuntarily collapse on the floor.

Shane would make me feel more secure because I knew that he knew everything about my care because he was with me through every therapy, every doctor's visit, and all the warnings about safety. I depended on him for everything. He continued to show me Christ every day, and I have been so very grateful. His strength came directly from God because I was too pitiful to ever give him anything but a "thank you."

One day, while contemplating this stressful situation, I was reminded of an old movie that my sister and I watched titled *To Sir with Love* because it contained a song about how thankful the star was because she had a particular teacher in her life. It said, "How do you thank someone who has taken you from crayons to perfume..." I would always cry at that point in the movie, and now relating to this song in a whole new way, it still brings tears to my eyes. I knew that I would never feel like I could repay Shane for all he was doing. Our roles were reversed, and I had become the child submitting to my son's care and requests, a child that I could once hold with one hand and kiss his sweet cheeks, now caring for me and waiting to hear my every breath. He told me after I got home that he couldn't sleep nights for fear that I needed him or I wasn't breathing. That sounded all too familiar. Shane doesn't allow me to cry. I only got one per day, and often, that just wasn't enough. But his encouragement has kept me from deep depression because when I think about what I have been through in the past two years, I get very sad. Even though I have never forgotten that God still has a plan and He is with me, my own sin sometimes hides His face and fear or pity, things that are not of God, overtake me, and I focus on the circumstances that I am commanded to rise above. Sometimes it's hard for me to understand it all. I felt like a desperate, helpless child again. I wanted someone to just hold me and give me a reasonable explanation why all of this was happening. I always felt so guilty that Shane was in this difficult position because of me and the fact that Mike worked every night just to keep insurance. I never dreamed that at this stage of my life, I would be such a burden or that Mike would feel so alone in caring for me.

9

The Church

Shane later told me that while I was being revived, the entire family had gathered around me to pray. No longer able to watch the attempts at resuscitation and hear the opinions of onlookers about whether I could make it after going forty-one minutes without a pulse or heartbeat, he fled to his safe place, Whitesburg Baptist Church, where he was a vital part of a strong youth ministry years earlier. Since this all occurred on a Sunday morning, a dear friend, Joyce Calvert, was there to greet him as he literally ran into her arms, sobbing. Thank God for her and the many others that ministered to him on that day and to my family in the days to come.

While on the ventilator, even though I was not conscious, I could recognize certain voices but could not recall what was said. I heard and knew the voices of my children and husband. One night, while in this induced sleep, I saw heaven—not like I was there, but from the outside looking in. While viewing heaven, I saw Nan-naw, my grandmother, who had passed away a year earlier. She had always encouraged me with the scriptures. She was sitting at the top of a golden circular staircase. It was a kind of gold that I had never seen before. It was not a color in this world. It was the brightest gold that I have ever witnessed and instantly I recognized that it was indeed heaven. Nan-Naw said, "Slow your breathing down." She continued to say that over and over.

Then I spotted my stepfather, who had also passed, standing on the top of the stairwell behind her. He kept telling me to get up. He had a debilitating stroke that he made little recovery from, so I knew that he knew exactly how I was feeling, and he did not want me to stop trying. I was relieved when I saw him since I didn't have to pretend anymore. He knew it all and could truly relate to my pain like no one else. I remember knowing that I was seeing them in heaven because I felt their sincere encouragement for me and their joy for being in the presence of Christ. I felt elated to see them and could recognize them both as if they were standing in my room. In fact, I questioned that they may be standing at the foot of my bed.

There were a few books written at that time about visiting heaven in a different sense than what I was experiencing, but I know that when I actually go there, God's word teaches that I would never want to leave His glorious presence. I was not in that glorious place, only witnessing some who were. I know this because I clearly still felt like I had to be here on earth and had some unfinished business that I was expected to take care of, *This Book* for one. I knew that He was telling me to write, something that I have always dreamed of doing.

I felt I had to see so many people again if only to thank them for impacting my Christian walk. My husband did not want to lose me even though he had no idea of the trials yet to come and how they would change us all. He would try his best to comfort me and tried so hard to make me see that God had a purpose even though we did not understand it right now. Shane was back from church in time to hear the news from ER that I had a heartbeat and was ready to come off the ventilator. One miracle among many yet to come. Thank you, Jesus, for never leaving or forsaking me no matter how dark and lonely it got. God allowed me to continue a life with everyone I love, and I am forever grateful. He spoke to me for many days while I lie in a hospital bed. He said, "Hear my voice when I call. Seek my face. I'm certain I will see the Lord's goodness. Be courageous. Let your heart be strong. Wait on the Lord."

I was not able to communicate due to the tracheotomy, and my mind was incapable of understanding everything that was happening most of the time. I felt like I was on the outside of most conversations, unable to get a grasp of what was going on. I struggled thinking that my mind was okay but not really being able to understand much or remember anything. My daughter told me later that while I was in the emergency room, my husband, Shane, and herself held hands and prayed over me that no matter how hard it would be for them to lose me, they wanted God's will to be done, whether I went to be with Him or remain with them. She said that as hard as it was to pray those words, her daddy mouthed them in a beautiful prayer to our Lord.

I later took much encouragement knowing that my family was not as selfish to pray that I would remain if it were not God's perfect will; this tells me that He indeed still had a plan for keeping me here.

I just awakened to discover that I had been through some very tough days, which I had no remembrance of. I learned that I was taken off the life support, and my family was encouraged that things were looking much better. I later learned that my family had spent a lot time in the chapel. It was so strange to learn all of this information with no real recollection of what had been going on. Most of my family was there, some traveling a great distance, and many friends from the many churches that we were affiliated with, as we were busy planting a new ministry outside of Huntsville and had served in several other ministries through the years.

I am so thankful for the church; many family members commented that this was a true representation of the New Testament church in action. This church responded exactly like Christ instructed us to. They provided for my family's needs, encouraging me with prayer and visits. I was selling real estate for Keller Williams who also responded with love and care for our needs, and I am so thankful for so many of the most wonderful agents.

It seemed like every TV show and even the commercials reminded me of all the things I would never be able to do again. I am such a realist that I struggled with finding all the new things I would be able to do. The commercials always showed babies that I did not have in my life and reminded me that I may never have or live to see grandchildren. It is so easy to become consumed with the sad thoughts; I now understand why so many people cop out and blame depression, turning to drugs for some kind of comfort; that would have been much easier, for sure. That is definitely the easiest way, sleep verses suffering. To fight, it is just that, a fight, daily and never ending.

You have to choose every moment of every day to be happy. You have to trust God so that you can find contentment because peace only comes from knowing Him. I know that this is a struggle that I may continue to have for a very long time, always feeling like I have lost so much and have taken so many down with me. But in order to be the overcomer that Christ wants for me, according to the book of Revelation, I have to rise above it. I have to allow myself to be saddened at times, but I cannot give in to pity.

After all, I was once a pastor's wife, full of endless energy, selling real estate with the most wonderful people in the world and loving every minute of it (especially closings). Finally, my dear friend Susan told me all about the road to where I was, how everything happened, who were there and all of the responses on social media to her reports about my status. I began to understand how wrong my depression was and that I had to be stronger because He who began a good work in me would be faithful to complete it, and I was not complete. Thank you, Susan Jackson, for always giving me encouraging truth. I was soon moved to the ICU where I was allowed more individual attention.

I had a hard time with understanding it all but was told that my mother, father, and stepmother were all staying at a house provided by the hospital for the family of their patients, and we were all so grateful. My dad must have been busy making friends because it wasn't long before he told me that he had been asked to be the guest speaker at a fundraising dinner they were having for the house they were staying in. I was so proud of him and very sorry that I was unable to attend and hear him, so I made him practice his speech with me.

It wasn't long that they told me that I would be moving to the center for rehabilitation. I had a purpose, and it made me very excited to look forward to something. I knew that Shane believed I could do it if I just kept getting up. I revisited my heavenly dream many times throughout the day, thankful that God would allow them to speak wisdom into my life and encourage me so much. I struggled to urinate but found it easier when the TV was showing something with water. *Wipe Out* was the most encouraging show but was not always on when I needed it. Sometimes it helped to run a trickle of water, and I had to be left alone. Each time I had a new tech, it was like a whole new training session, and I got to the point where I dreaded any new people coming into my room because of my necessary rituals. I was so much more comfortable with those that knew my routine, but they changed every six hours regardless. I would try all the dumb high school party tricks and still have no urine many times, giving me just another thing to worry and dread about. Many times, they would catheterize me just to empty my bladder. I have excessive urination today but often have trouble getting it started, probably because of these very issues. Everything had a side effect.

I was always glad to see my trach doctor because he was tall, dark, and always smiling every time I saw him. I told him that I wanted to take the trach out and to have a big glass of ice water. He said, "Well, I want a pink pony that poops dollar bills too, but sometimes, we don't get what we want." After laughing, I asked him if he knew Jesus Christ, explaining that all things are possible with Him. I told him to hang on to the hope, because I was. I don't know what happened with the pony because we never discussed it again. I was still wearing many tubes because I had such a weak heart and was in need of breathing treatments twice a day.

My trach doctor checked on me often and soon became my favorite doctor who visited. As I awaited the day for the trach to be removed, they fitted me for a special piece to place in my throat that closed off the hole, enabling me to speak. It did not sound like my voice, but at least I could try to communicate without my white board. Taylor said that I sounded like Darth Vader and a dinosaur rolled into one. My mom would make me wear it to talk to her; I don't think she thought I would ever talk again. I was encouraged to use it several hours every day, and at first, I was excited; however, the excitement wore off quickly because it was so uncomfortable when it was in place. I would quickly resort back to my white board, which was more comfortable.

After several weeks of using the new throat stopper to talk, I was told that they were getting closer to removing the trach. I was elated until my doctor told me how it's done. It sounded painful, and it was, but the thought of liquid going down my throat made it come about with no fear. Soon enough, he granted my wish and literally ripped the trach from my throat. The main thing that I remember about these days was my thirst; I had gone for weeks without being able to swallow or drink anything. It was horrible. My teeth would stick to my lips, making me want to continue to lie in bed, doing nothing except thinking about how badly all of my illness had affected my poor family. My mouth was sore inside because of the dryness.

I remember having a swallowing test done next where they fed me several things to establish what consistency I could tolerate, starting with a sugar-free grape popsicle; nothing has ever tasted that good to me. The cold liquid in my dry, thirsty mouth was everything I dreamed it would be, and believe me, I had dreamed about it. It was all I could think about. I was so thirsty.

This test established that I would have to have my liquids thickened somewhat, and I could not drink with a straw. They would pour a dry packet of thickener into my water and every drink I had. It would become the consistency of V8 juice, which began a healthy relationship between myself and this drink of choice. I even took my pills every morning with V8 over ice. The reasoning as I understand it was so that it would go down correctly and not end up in my lungs. I got very used to the thickened liquids but still craved a huge glass of ice water without the thickener, to be honest.

I knew that I entered this journey not by choice but for a reason. I thought about it day and night and prayed that God would give me answers so that I would not miss one opportunity that He would give me to impact someone's life for Him. My special adopted mom and dad, Bonnie and JR, visited me nearly every day and continued to encourage me to write my story. They were simple Christian neighbors who adopted us and helped us in so many ways while we lived on their street. They were our family away from family and never treated us with anything but love. Great people that do great things and we were so blessed to have them. I feel like I owe them so much for always being there for us.

Since the hospital food was unseasoned and much of the same thing over and over, I did not eat much, and when I tried, I did not enjoy it at all. My family was there to encourage me to eat the protein to help me heal, so at least I had an undercooked, unseasoned scrambled egg every morning. That was something to look forward to.

After a trip to Panera Bread to bring me a craved spinach soufflé, Mike reminded me that "this is not where I belong," a line from the new song he heard on the radio. He then read me the life of Joseph and Psalm 27:1, where David goes from faith to fear in his life. He says when we are living in faith, even our enemies cannot touch us. Fear had certainly become my enemy. War breaks out against me. I want to dwell in the house of the Lord all the days of my life. How can you have such a mood swing in just one Psalm? This brought me much comfort as I felt like I had many mood swings each day as well, and I took joy from David. A journey like the one I have had can certainly steal your joy, and without constant encouragement, depression is only a thought away. Many people were there to offer me encouragement, and I know that they were all a part of God's provision.

Since my mother lived in Kentucky and my father in Florida, I knew they would not be there long after I began to improve, and I knew that I had to make them know how much I loved them for the life they had given me and all the choices they steered me to make. I could not move well all the time and was consumed with the feeling that I had to make sure that my relationships knew what they meant to me and how thankful I was for each of them. I often doubted that I would continue to live, thinking I was so undeserving. Even though I knew I was a miracle, I had a strange desire to make sure I said good-bye and shared my love with so many. A part of me was so grateful while another darker side thought that everyone else would be so much better off if I could just go and be with Christ. My family reminded me that I couldn't play God's role trying to decide when I should go be with Him. He knew when, and at this time he wanted me to win, but like salvation, I had to choose to win this. The road would not be an easy one. I did not even imagine at that time that it could get as difficult as it did.

Bonnie always said that I should write my story because all that I had gone through was so unbelievable. No matter how bad it got, she was always there to encourage me. She and JR even accompanied me to therapy one day and cheered me on as I struggled to walk.

Mike came faithfully every night and would read to me from the Bible, either from Job or the life of Joseph. He meant to encourage me to trust the Lord the way these men did, but it sometimes made me feel like more of a failure, thinking that I could not measure up. I had so many people telling me how strong I was and how convinced they were that I could get through this. But I could not see it. I felt like a hypocrite, thinking I would never be able to get through all of this. At times, I would feel so sorry because of what this had done to my family. I began to ask God why He didn't just let me die.

My oldest son, Jared, had been in and out of our lives in the last few years as he was dealing with the consequences of some very poor choices. He was in my prayers daily for the past twenty-five years, praying that God would give him wisdom and bring him back into our lives on a more regular basis, mending the relationships that needed to be rejuvenated. He works for a graphics company and travels all over building graphic signs at golf tournaments, so his schedule is crazy. He told me that he was in Boston working when he got a call informing him that I may not live through the night, so he caught a plane, and here he was. He was careful not to commit to a timeframe, but I was so happy to see him and enjoyed every moment with him in this boring hospital. Between him and Shane, they had all the female techs swooning and visiting my room more often. Both of my boys are quite handsome and look quite similar, confusing many. Since I was completely dependent on someone to take me to the restroom, Shane was glad to see Jared as well, giving him a break from potty duty. Jared was faithful and would sleep in my recliner and tell me all the things I wanted and needed to hear during the day. God gave me a huge, strong husband and two strong sons for this reason; they had to lift me everywhere that I moved.

The painkiller of choice at this hospital was morphine, and as much as I was afraid to ask for it, I could not sleep without it. So every night I had 2 cc of morphine administered through my IV, and I could actually feel it as it moved from my hand up my arm and through my body, completely knocking me out. When I questioned my nurses, they assured me that I was not taking enough to hurt me or cause addiction. That was not true. Night after night, I had to have it to sleep, and I was happy to follow orders because I had not really slept in so long. I began to look forward to bedtime, which had been a nightmare before morphine. I questioned why I couldn't have a pain pill of some kind but was told that morphine or Tylenol were my only ordered forms of pain meds.

Pity is never pretty or God-honoring, but I was consumed with the sorrow I was causing for so many. My younger sister and brother were counting on me to be the overcomer that I had been so often. I wanted so badly not to disappoint anyone, but no one seemed to understand how difficult this was in my head. I truly wanted to quit, and I remember calling of my children to say good-bye, just in case I did not draw another breath because I was convinced it would be easier for everyone if I didn't.

I began to struggle to breathe as I was being told to sleep, wishing it were that easy. I was moved to the rehabilitation facility attached to the hospital and was put on a small amount of oxygen at night in hopes I could sleep. The television was always on, and every commercial seemed to be about quenching a thirst with some delicious-looking beverage. It was bad enough what this stroke had done to my existence, but I couldn't bear to think about what it was doing to my husband, children, and parents. I knew that all of them loved me so much and would have traded places if possible, but I knew that I did not choose this. There was a reason I was the one that was on this journey, so my family would have to endure it as I did.

Another thing that no one ever discussed with me was the possibility of dehydration. They did say to watch my urine and assure that it is not turning brown, but oftentimes, I had very brown urine. My teeth were breaking off and chipping all over my mouth; I later learned that this was a side effect of dehydration. Of course, I may never be able to justify getting any of them fixed because of the hundreds of thousands of dollars that I already owe the medical community. I was never worth this kind of money even in my best days. Smiling became less and less of an option as my teeth continued to crack and fall out of my mouth. My smile was always a good part of me; after all, it earned me a spot in the choir, and now I would rather not smile at all.

I quickly allowed Satan to fill my heart with pity instead of praise. God had spared my life and kept my brain functioning throughout a horrible time of breathlessness. I knew that I should be overjoyed, but it was so hard for me to remember how to do that. My heart was not pumping at a normal rate, so I had been knocked out for days, but I still had hope. The actual stroke pain, which they called toning, was awfully painful, making it difficult for me to sleep because I could never find a comfortable position due to the stroke. Sleep was a treasured gift that I still struggle to take hold of.

After thirty-two years of marriage, I celebrated our anniversary in the hospital. I was unaware and disappointed to see how little Mike really knew me because of all the questions he asked in order to make me more comfortable. All the simple things that I assumed he would know about me, like I never drink anything without ice or I hated to brush my teeth in the shower. He did not know. It was amazing how important all the little things become when you have nothing to do but think. I really wanted him to know things without asking. I wanted him to know that I wanted ketchup on my scrambled eggs, not because he could ask me, but because I have always had them that way and he noticed.

I believe that noticing is the key. Every woman wants to believe that all the things that are important to her are noticed and even appreciated by her spouse. I tried not to focus on this as I was still trying to fix my daughter up with someone, and I was running out of prospects. Every male there was married or didn't love Jesus.

I was very encouraged when one of my favorite techs, Paul, told me his love story. He was in a pizza place at Auburn University when he looked at this girl, and instantly he knew that he had to approach her and get to know who she was. He paid for her pizzas, and that was the beginning of a beautiful love relationship. Two years later, they were married and expecting their first child.

I was encouraged that it could still happen for Taylor even though she has such a high standard. It may take a while. I needed to just be patient and let God work it all out. I did not want her to ever compromise her standard, but I was consumed with the thought of living long enough to see my kids married and producing a family of their own and seeing them happy like we were. Patience is something that I struggled with, so here's another opportunity for me. It still amazed me that He continued to allow me to learn and grow in my faith.

It did not take long before they moved me to the rehab hospital again. I was determined to be the best I could be each day. My immediate family went with me. I was warned that because it was a weekend, not much would be happening as far as therapy or anything. I was disappointed but did my best to hide it as the on-call doctor questioned me. I told my mother that I was feeling really sick and strange and I was unsure why. I threw up and got chills. I was sweating furiously, and my heart was racing. They sent me back to the hospital. After looking back, I was assured that I was having withdrawal from the morphine, which would probably mean no sleep for me at rehab. My family was critical of the move, but I was glad to be moving in the direction of walking again; it was all I could think about.

I had an endocrinologist managing my sugar levels. I had controlled my sugars with an insulin pump at home, but they did not allow it in the hospital; therefore, my sugars were out of control. They would go from a 300 to a 45, scaring the staff into a massive feeding of whatever they could get me to eat. It was rough dealing with all of this. My heart was much too weak to handle all that was wrong with me. I had to try to be a good patient because I had never depended on anyone but the Lord before all of this, and it was so difficult.

One more week here did not even seem possible as my butt was in tremendous pain from this bed. Due to the uncontrollable sugars and all the trauma, I was thirsty all of the time, drinking a ton of water. The breathing treatments continued three times every day and at what seemed like the most inconvenient times. This place and the new drugs and the routines were my new life, and no matter how I felt about all of it, it really didn't matter. I just did what I was told and tried to be as good as I possibly could, and no matter how hard I tried not to let it, I was totally dependent on someone else for everything, maybe so that I might realize that I did not understand total dependency like I thought I did. God had to have control of all of it and deserved my trust.

The battles raged on in my mind every day and through most nights, making laughter the farthest thing from my mind. I would sometimes be caught off guard by a face from the past that would visit and make me smile. When you are stuck in a hospital, it is wonderful to have those surprising visits. One day, during a visit, my dear friend Susan Jackson gave me her perspective of all that had gone on while I was out. She had created a Facebook page, keeping everyone who cared informed of my status. I know that all of these prayer warriors have no idea, but God was using them and their prayers, and they were getting me through.

Moving back to rehab again, this time the doctor encouraged me to stay away from narcotics but still find a way to sleep. My mom was with me, and we decided that I had to do something in order to be strong enough for therapy. He told us about people taking Benadryl at bedtime. I decided to give it a try. I slept with no problem. The problem was that I slept all night but wanted to continue sleeping the whole next day. It knocked me out. My PT, who was a fireball, tried very hard to keep me awake, so I promised her I would not take it again. She would work me hard, which is what I needed. And again, I was grateful. I loved being back in rehab even though I struggled so hard to stay awake that first day back. I was so confident that rehab was going to allow me to get my body back.

My mom, who also sacrificed and stayed with me for a very long time, accompanied me to therapy this day. She was also having a difficult time entertaining me enough to keep my eyes open; however, she was a great cheerleader and truly made me want to do better just because she was there. She was leaving at the end of the week, so I wanted her to be assured that I was going to make it, knowing that I was in good hands with my PT.

10

Tammy

I will never forget meeting my physical therapist, Tammy. I instantly knew that God had chosen her for me. She had a reputation of being the toughest, but she was the best, and her attitude was perfect for me. I loved that she was serious about rehab but fun at the same time.

She told me that I needed to name my arm. I had to think of a man's name that I didn't really like so we would have something to call him. So I called my arm Eugene, a person I loved but whose name I had no taste for. Then one day, during a workout, she referred to my leg as Taco. So Taco and Eugene became famous in the rehab room, and believe it or not, Taco responded much better when referred to by name.

Tammy pushed me and did it always with encouragement and even love. I began to love her like my own child and thanked God for her each day as I struggled to do everything she required of me, never wanting to disappoint her in any way. Breathing treatments continued, and they told me they were helping, but I couldn't feel any difference and the coughing was the same. I finally had a day where I was feeling well. I credited it to a little Activia and the fact that I got a call from my best friend in the world who lives in Colorado, informing me that she and her amazing husband were coming to visit me on Saturday.

I had not seen them for six years, and to say I was excited did not do my feelings justice. I got to take a day pass and go to the park and out to eat with our friends. She is always on my mind and in my prayers, and to be with her again made me joyful again. She was the kind of friend that made suggestions to me about God having a plan for my life that may contradict my own. When I moved to Virginia many years earlier, Cindy was one of those women in my first Bible tudy who encouraged me with many scriptures. While I was looking for a job, she suggested that God possibly wanted me to focus on staying home and raising my three-year-old son, instead of allowing strangers in a day care to raise him. That decision and my relationship with her changed and encouraged my life, leading me into true motherhood, depending on our Lord in every decision I made.

Everyone fell in love with Tammy, and we all trusted that I would walk again. My oldest son showed up and made therapy a whole new experience as he is always so entertaining. When he learned that we were calling my leg Taco, he began singing the song, "Taco, burritos, what's coming out of your Speedos, you got troubles, you're blowing bubbles." He would repeat it over and over again trying to distract me to the point of laughter, and I would always laugh. Sometimes I wonder where he came from, with his likeability and wonderful sense of humor. I saw huge improvement as I moved my foot voluntarily. I was tremendously hopeful. Making memories with my boys were what these days were all about, and even though it was not what I would have chosen, it got me through many tough days and onto another night

Every time a new physician came into my room, he or she would ask me if I ever had thoughts of suicide. I knew that "no" was the appropriate answer, but at times, I day dreamed about what it would be like for everyone if I could just stop breathing. We were not wealthy, and I knew that the expenses were in the hundreds of thousands of dollars. I was worried about how we could ever recover. We didn't. I never told anyone this, but I often thought that it would really be the best thing for everyone if I could just go to sleep and not wake up. A nurse once told me that depression is so common in stroke patients; they have to ask about suicidal thoughts as it is always a huge risk. I always responded with the Christian answers, sometimes pretending that I had peace about this whole situation—when in reality, I had none. I just badly wanted someone to be able to understand the horror of this process. It felt as if I went to sleep and awoke in someone else's body, a very old, sick, and ugly one.

I had such a fear of being alone, and I had no understanding of it at all. I was never afraid of anything except snakes and my dad's whippings, not even death scared me because of my assurance of going to be with Jesus. But I could not discern why I was so afraid other than wanting so badly to be there to see my children mature and have families and happiness. Due to all of my medical complications, I did not believe that it could be done, but I knew that the Lord was with me and would continue to comfort me. It was a battle that was very strange to me but was there just the same. Shane continued to endure his commitment to stay by me, reminding me often of how good God had been to me, even though it was so hard on him. Mike was working at night and could not manage to be there except after he got off at five o'clock. He had to continue to work in order to keep our insurance paying for me to stay in the hospital. I didn't understand that at times and was hard on him because of it, but he felt like he had no choices in any of this. I was being selfish and wanted his comfort so much. When you face death that closely, it just changes things—no not just things, it changes everything.

11

Froggie Went a Courtin'

Taylor must have called my dad and told him that I was sad because it wasn't long before I got a call saying that he was coming back to see me. It was an exciting day when my dad came back to stay with me. I was so happy to see him, realizing that I have never done loneliness well. I felt bad that he had to make such a long trip, but I was selfish enough to live with it.

My father is an avid reader, and he began to read his book to me every day aloud, giving me a much-needed break from TV. I got very involved in the espionage and intrigue of his latest novel. Poppa, my dad, stayed with me several nights, allowing Shane to rest at home, and I was so thankful. Since my parents divorced when I was young, I had fewer memories of my dad than most. Even though I spent every weekend at his house, he and my stepmother stayed busy.

My dad and I went to the common area, a large sun-filled room, and worked on jigsaw puzzles until we had completed every one that they had to offer. Even though he could always find the piece I couldn't, I really enjoyed this time with him. This was therapeutic for me to feel like I was accomplishing something, even if it was a flower basket with birds or a weird-looking frog.

Each time we would open a new box and begin to find the edge pieces, I was reminded of my Nan-naw, who always had a puzzle set up at her house and taught me how to find the appropriate pieces at a young age. I loved that the void feelings in my mind were beginning to fill with memories I was familiar with. The puzzles occupied my mind with something other than my own struggles.

The one thing I remember more than anything else is a silly song that he always sang to me. It was called "Froggie Went a Courtin'." Even though he said he had forgotten it, together we came up with the tune, and the words all came back to us. He sang this song to me, and I felt like a loved child again, making it easier for me to relax.

Most of the time, I felt it was impossible to really rest because my mind was so busy thinking about all that was going on and wondering how anything was ever going to work again. Nothing about my life or me was the same. I had little memories that were my own, but the whole incident was told to me from different people and perspectives because I had absolutely no memory of it at all. I just worked hard to make sense of all the stories I was given and tried to remember that I was indeed a part of what they were telling me.

We had just bought a house, which I had not been to except a brief walk through, and the stress of moving without being able to pack myself was overwhelming as well. I sold real estate and had many clients waiting for me to introduce them to their wonderful new homes. I tried to get agents in my office to take on my clients, but it was all so difficult in my condition. We had moved many times before, but never without me packing and giving orders as to where everything should go and how it should be unpacked. No, I do not struggle with power issues; I am just very experienced at moving.

I couldn't stand to admit or think about it, but people who met me during these days would have described me as sad, even pitiful. And knowing that made me feel even sadder. I finally realized that I was the only one that could break this vicious cycle. I was still saddened due to so little understanding, I had to stop looking at myself. This was when I finally got my prayer life back and knew that I was responsible for what I filled my mind with. It was easier to blame my circumstances than accepting the responsibility myself. Prayer became my restful place from then on and got me beyond many painful days. Since I always had some fluid in my lungs, I was never found without my Kleenex, much to my kids' embarrassment. I always had one tucked somewhere just in case a coughing fit hit me. I spit and blew a lot, not something to be proud of, but it just comes with the trial. God was good even in the little things.

When you are blessed enough to have the kind of friends that I have, not just speaking the words but putting action to them and truly praying, it matters. I felt the power of prayer often, most of the time, when I would struggle so hard to sleep. I was so grateful when I could imagine so many of my friends and family on their knees, praying to God on my behalf. It is a very humbling experience.

12

Strokes Hurt

All I could think about was how bad it was not to be able to use my whole left side. The pain was strange; it traveled up and down my left side like tingling spikes, bringing me to tears often. Strokes just hurt. As I laid in pain or under the influence of strong medication, I thought about so many things, but the more I thought about my situation, the more depressed I became. But I know this was not who I was, making me even sadder that I was allowing all of this emotion to dominate my spirit. Going through this type of trial will give you plenty of time to truly evaluate your relationship with the Lord.

Mike would remind me with stories from the Bible hoping to make me feel stronger. For instance, David, after committing sin with Bathsheba, allowed his sin to bring him to a contrite spirit. I know that God's plan in our every trial is that we endure it, meaning, gird up under it and allow perseverance to be the final result so that we might be perfect or lacking in nothing. I have to look forward to that day, hoping that my reactions may encourage someone else. I knew where to turn when I felt weak. I just could not get there. It was like going somewhere that you have been to before, but you could no longer remember the details of actually pulling into the drive. At times I can even see the house and the details of the hedges but cannot reach it. Therefore, I felt as if I had all of this stuff so bottled up inside of me that I needed to just regurgitate it all out in order to ever get beyond it. But I felt like I had no one strong enough to allow me to do that. I had to be the strong one. I always was.

The Lord Himself was the only one I had to go to, so why did I allow Satan to speak so many lies into my head that I couldn't even break down with Jesus. I had no idea, but I had nurses, friends, and techs tell me that each day I needed to think of one positive thought and just think about that every time I would feel sad. I did that. I thought about Siesta Key and the beauty and fun of the beach that we went to every year with our kids and our dear friends. God would give me a scripture every day, either through a card from Susan Fields, a visit, some flowers, or a Facebook message that would get me through to a new day.

I felt so guilty that I would no longer be able to minister to my family because it was the best thing I ever did, and my physical condition would no longer allow it. I mourned every time I would think about all that I would no longer be able to do. I just wanted something to be easy. It was difficult peeing, pooping, chewing, talking, eating, reading, focusing, and sleeping. I wanted to do something easy, at least just one. It finally came to me: praying for others became my "easy thing."

I remember my friend Susan telling me that my face was not as saggy as it was the week before, so I assume the stroke made my left side droop in the beginning. That explained why I had trouble chewing at first, biting my jaws often. Today, I feel like my face just looks old more than the result of the stroke. When I get emotional or when I sleep in certain positions, I drool sometimes, but nothing life-changing when you have as much going on as I do. A little slobber is nothing. This kind of trauma sure puts things in perspective.

One of my most embarrassing and memorable moments at rehab occurred after Mike talked me into drinking a cup of warm prune juice from the day room. I finally got it down about the time that Juanita came in and told me that she was going to the second floor to get her special shower chair, which was made of PVC pipes and had a toilet seat on it. She sat me on the pottie to try once again to poop. I was finally able to go, so after celebrating with me, she moved me directly onto her special shower chair and pushed me into my bathroom. I looked at Mike in terror and asked him to get me a paper towel to poop in. He refused, and after she rolled me into the shower, she handed me a washcloth and told me to wash my backside. You can imagine my surprise when I felt a huge turd sticking out of me. I told her what was happening as I handed her three turds in the washcloth. Then as she wheeled me around, I saw another turd in the drain and still felt like I could go again. She was not laughing as she put me back on the potty to finish. I began to slide forward so she pulled my panties but did not get them up thankfully because I unloaded everything I had. I really began to appreciate all that the techs do. That night, I vowed to show my appreciation to them every day from that moment on.

I feel like getting new glasses cleared so many things up for me. I really could not see at all before I got the new glasses. God has been so good to me in the little things, and I will never stop trying to get Eugene, my left arm, to wake up and help me carry this load. To think about your limb being unable to ever move is a foreign thought, but it has become a depressing reality. I know how much easier it will be to carry out the plan God has for me if I had two working arms and hands, so I work on it daily, hoping that one miraculous day, it will just remember what it is supposed to do and do it. The actual pain associated with the stretch has gotten much better as time has progressed, but I still have no voluntary movement anywhere in my arm, shoulder, or hand.

Mike read Job to me often, and I was reminded that he lost everything, yet he never doubted his faith in God. I knew that somehow I had to get back to that place where I knew beyond any doubt that God had a purpose even though I could not see it. I had to trust that He would work everything out for good, and He was going to get the glory. I have never wanted anything like I wanted to glorify God through all of this; of course, I perceived that to be me walking and becoming independent again.

I wanted to begin building up my muscles, and I assumed that it would be weeks before I would get back in order to start rehab.

I had always loved exercise and so looked forward to getting to do more. I had so much toning in my arm that it was so painful to move or even touch it. When I would try to roll to my side, my arm would get stuck and become very painful; then I would try to sit up, realizing that I was sitting on Eugene. More pain.

The first occupational therapist that I had was not very aggressive and bored me so much with the same simple activity. I blamed her that my toning was not improving. I went to speech therapy, even though it was my least favorite, and I really couldn't see well enough to do many of her activities. I did not discover until many months later that the stroke had badly affected my left eye and my vision was horrible, keeping me from reading or accomplishing any of the things like I once had. I wanted so badly to continue in therapy, believing this was the answer, forgetting that the Lord is always the answer. Fluid in my lungs was another enemy that I was battling and losing to. I was able to cough up mucus on an hourly basis; at least this was one thing I could always count on.

A friend showed up one day. Her name is Mary, a long-lost sorority sister from Yay Alpha Phi. She had taken a hard fall years earlier and experienced paralysis and had gone through rehab herself. She was the most encouraging because she could relate to my pain and the struggles of rehabilitating the body. Everyone would say, "Squeeze my hand," or "Lift up your leg," and I would think to myself, *You have no idea what this is like.* But my friend knew, and even though I was so sorry that she had gone through this, I was also grateful because finally someone could understand. My great friends from Atlanta, Cheri and Steve, were there as they always were whenever I was struggling. They also offered me so much support and laughter. My friend Susan, who created that Facebook page when I had my stroke and was pronounced DOA, kept the information going, keeping all my contacts informed of all I was going through, so I had prayers coming from all over the world as we had ministered in South America and Africa, Mexico, and Peru. I had met incredible people in all of these countries, working to plant churches. I had prayers going up every day, and I truly knew and felt them.

I began to look forward to moving to rehab to begin therapy because I truly believed that God is able. I was thrilled that this was not the final chapter because I knew that at any time, God could say, as He did to Lazarus, "Rise up and walk." I wanted so badly to believe it. I wish I could write that this is what happened, but I had a lot more to learn and more dependency to build evidently. So I remain in the wheelchair to this day, never giving up the hope.

A total restoration was my prayer; however, I have had an opportunity to see His power and personality. He still has a purpose and a plan for my life as He does for everyone, and I have truly learned that without His strength, I am nothing. I will continue as best I can to focus on the journey, keeping the promise of Jeremiah 29:11, "I know the plans I have for you declares the Lord, plans to prosper you, not to harm you and to give you a future and a hope." I had to keep these words in my mind, always praising Him and hoping to encourage someone else. So many people have encouraged me throughout this process.

As I thought about our latest puzzle, I dreamed about how God holds the pieces of our lives in His hands, much like the pieces to the puzzle. He adds pieces as we spiritually mature, careful to never give us more temptation than we can endure. As I looked at my life, it looked much like a scattered puzzle. I was so grateful that God was putting the pieces all together, not expecting me to. Even though I thought I knew where the pieces should go, I could never make the beautiful picture that He can. With that, I felt some relief. I was able to look to the future with excitement to see how He was going to complete my life puzzle so that it might give Him glory. In rehab once again, I was improving every day and was motivated that I would indeed walk again one day. Hope is the best thing to bring about another day; therefore, I tried to focus on any hopeful moment or thought.

I hated to leave my therapy, even though I wanted to be home with my family. I had many mixed emotions. For one reason, my husband had been busy working to maintain the insurance and getting friends to widen doors at our house and remodel bathrooms to accommodate my situation. This meant that he did not have a deep understanding of how my needs had changed. This meant missing out on learning how he can help me do my new daily activities. It was near impossible for him to see me go from what I was to what I had now become with acceptance. But even if that was the case, he remains faithful and encouraging.

It frightened me to be out of the hands of the professionals I was compelled to trust, not even understanding at the time what their neglect had done to me or what was about to come. I believed that surely the worst was over. Little did I know.

I tried not to bother anyone too often. I was on Lasix, which helped prevent swelling, so I had a mental schedule of when I could drink so that my pee time would not interfere with my therapy or anything else that I knew my day held. This problem began to really stress me out because I hated to call for help. This issue continued once I got out, even though Shane, my caregiver, was very used to it. I was so humbled to think about my sons having to pull down my pants allow me to pee then pull them back up again. I could hardly stand it. I was so grateful yet sorry at the same time that emotions were uncontrollable. Since both of my sons have a great sense of humor, they always made me feel better about all they had to do for me. Humility took on a whole new definition for me.

I was discharged from rehab, but Shane continued to work with me daily. I achieved walking up and down our driveway several times per day. Walking was the greatest feeling in the world, something that I had taken for granted for so long. I was so determined to do it that it felt amazing to finally achieve my goal. We joined a community center in order to use the pool, and Shane would get me walking on the bottom of the pool several times a week.

Money was tight due to so many medical expenses, but I still had enough therapy visits to do some outpatient therapy back at my rehab center. I worked with new therapists, Heather and Chelsea, but loved going and getting the work out just the same. My OT was awesome, and she got Eugene to move more than ever before through E-stem, electrical stimulation. I believe that if I had been given that earlier, my hand would have made a recovery, but I'm not a doctor.

I soon used up all the visits that insurance would allow, so it was back to Shane and myself. I had a sabo-stretch arm brace that I was supposed to wear to bed, but no one could get it to stay on right except Taylor, and she was not always there to get it on me. I remember at times that the stretch was so painful, I could not stand it throughout the night. So I would try to sneak out of it. The problem with that was that I always had to sleep with someone, and it had so many strong Velcro strips that it was very noisy coming off. I was afraid of waking Mike or Taylor, whichever stayed with me, so for fear of waking them, I would endure the pain. It would flatten out my otherwise curled hand by morning, so even though I hated the pain, I learned to stand it to achieve the results, a great description of why we do therapy to begin with. I always felt better having worn it, but Eugene was not liking the stretch.

My outpatient therapist recommended that I discuss taking a Botox injection in my arm for the toning, so it wasn't long that I was back in the doctor's office getting a Botox injection. It hurt a lot and did not really help Eugene out enough to get me excited about it, so I only had one injection there, and I was able to continue therapy. I was once again thrilled and couldn't wait to get started.

I tried so hard to do everything that they told me; however, looking back, it was never enough. The muscles and nerves on my left side no longer worked. I remember many times having to start at my shoulder and travel down my arm to locate my hand. The only knowledge of a prosthetic that I had, like most Americans, came from watching *Dancing with the Stars* or some other media presentation, all misguided.

As I started training with this awkward heavy leg, it makes me a little angry that America gets that impression, missing the time, pain, and disappointment of actually learning to walk on one. I began therapy again, and thanks to Shane, I was beginning to get the knack of the actual process. I had to focus on every move and hope that my muscles were able to pull it off, never being confident or quite sure that they could. It was all so different than when your mind connects without even thinking about it. It is quite a process. I struggled to remember that I had to start off on my prosthetic, swinging it forward, trying to land it on my heel, then rolling forward to the ball of my rubberized foot hiding inside my hideous Velcro tennis shoe.

After I got out of therapy, I looked everywhere to find an inexpensive flat surface that I could begin walking on, but there was nothing in Louisville that met that need. It was turning cold and threatening snow, which would make it impossible for me to walk. My husband was looking for another job in a warmer climate, blaming it on me needing a warmer climate to walk in. An opportunity came up in Bradenton, Florida, where my father and stepmother lived.

When I was released from rehab, Shane made me feel like he was so proud of me, and that was all I wanted to hear. I pushed myself through the pain and the failures because of him, and I was so grateful that he tried his best to understand as he encouraged me. I still ached for someone who could pretend even to understand, but there was no one. I realized that everyone in my family had their own problems consuming their time and energy and could not afford to hear mine. I always tried to turn the situation around, focusing on what I would do if I were in their shoes, causing me more pain than comfort, realizing that I would probably have a difficult time understanding it too had I not gone through it. But I think I have more of a caregiver mentality than some of my family members; plus my mother and father were getting too old to take care of me. One thing I have learned through all of this is you cannot wait for a disabled person to ask for the help. I realized better than anyone what a burden I had become and never wanted anyone to have to take that on. I tried very hard to be satisfied with what I was given, not wanting to ever ask for anything. I admire and am even in awe of many graceful individuals in nursing homes and full-time care facilities that can be happy and appear satisfied because I'm not sure I could do it, and I pray I don't have to.

I was walking pretty good using a one-sided walker. I was even able to climb the stairs they had in the rehab room when I left, which really helped once I got home. I had to get in my front door with my daughter, who was unable to pull me up the steps in the chair. The boys just turned the chair around backwards and leaned me back and pulled, but it was too heavy and awkward for Taylor, so we laughed and climbed our way in several times when no one else was there. It only made me more aware of the importance of having a plan to assure that I was not an overwhelming burden. I needed a plan, and I knew how important that would be for my life from now on. They poked fun at me, but I believed that it was especially necessary for me now to always have a plan, something that someone with two arms and two legs could not possibly understand because they don't have to, and it is not a lesson voluntarily learned; it takes being forced to.

During my therapies, someone told me to establish a routine and try not to vary. I had several reservations, knowing that my family did not have a routine, but I did everything spur of the moment, so I knew that it would be more difficult for me since I had to plan every pee in my mind to assure that I would be at a place that would accommodate me and a helper, who was usually a male. My husband and, through heredity, my sons did not ever have a plan. The stress of being so dependent was overwhelming, but no one wanted to hear anything I had to say about it because I could not talk without tearing up and making those around me sad. When I tried to talk on the phone, I would blubber, making it impossible to be understood, so everyone gave up trying to talk to me, which I completely understood and wished could have been different. I could never remember a time in my life that I needed to talk to someone more than now, but it only became another impossibility among the many I already struggled with.

I was always big on not letting the sun go down on my anger before this, but that no longer had any value. I often went to bed mad and sad. Now that I had a voice, I just wanted someone to listen and even better to try to understand. I really needed a tight long hug. It was so humiliating to have to depend on my son the way I did as I knew it was difficult for him to be in this new position, one that you can't ever be prepared for. I still had some mind control issues, couldn't remember the short-term events well, and really struggled with numbers and anything associated with them. I could not even remember my new address or use my new fangled phone. No wonder no one wanted to talk to me about everything that was going on.

Each of my family members were dealing with my loss in their own way, and it was not easy for any of us.

My spouse had never been dependent on anyone since childhood, so I could not blame him for not understanding, but I did anyway. Everyone was hard on Mike, me included, and it was not justified because he was killing himself to do what was best for me.

Things were coming along nicely, Mike was working hard every day and returning home in the evenings to whatever dinner my kids had come up with. Shane and Jared are both great cooks, and Taylor, bless her heart, could make scrambled eggs and French toast. She was the brunt of many cooking jokes at our house. God has been so good to me in that I have had so many family and friends with me on this journey. I really don't want to let any of them down by not being an overcomer. Even though this feels like a marathon, I feel like I have so many in this race with me, and I found so much hope in that. I knew it was all about the journey, but I also know that Paul, in his letter to the Hebrews in particular, teaches us about how we finish, so as I look to the finish line, I want to be able to give more of Jesus away as I progress.

I still felt very alone in how to deal with it all myself. I should have had some professional assistance, but I wasn't wise enough to even realize it. We all suffered through with no conversation about what had happened to us all. My children tried very hard to make it easy on me, and Mike continued to work, doing all he could, with little help or appreciation.

13

Oh, What a Day

Shane kept me working out as much as possible until on the evening of February 14. I was back wearing my insulin pump when all of a sudden it was not administering my basil rate insulin properly. My sugar would not go down no matter how much I would bolus, and while sitting in my wheelchair in the living room, I began to have chest pain and feel very sick. My husband called my heart doctor, and he said to take me to the hospital. Bad mistake in hindsight. If I could have even imagined the outcome of this stay, I would have just died in my own living room. My husband, son, and daughter took me to the ER at the all-too-familiar hospital, my home away from home, thinking that I was having another heart attack. Of course, it was Valentine's Day. Since I had a habit of ruining every holiday for the past year, it wasn't surprising.

When we arrived and I had answered the million questions they ask, I remember the nurse in ER being very excited about a new bed sore patch. Due to my stroke, the staff discussed putting this new patch on my left heel. A nurse said they had just come from a conference where it was introduced, and it was supposed to protect me from getting a bed sore. I had no experience with these sores, but remember thinking, *Anything they are this excited about must be a good thing.* So I consented. She peeled a paper backing off of it and applied it to my heel. They ran many tests and heart scans and later moved me to the fifth floor. By this time, my sugar was so high, I was in keto-acidosis and dealing with the possibility of a diabetic coma.

My son and husband were with me. I warned all the nurses not to pull on Eugene, my arm, because he did not like it. As I lay in the very uncomfortable yet too familiar bed, I began to feel like there was something sore on my heel under the protection pad they had put on me. I asked the nurse to look at it, but I was told that if they put it on me in the ER, she could not take it off. Therefore, no one would look at my heel. I spent a week in the hospital, complaining several times and being told the same thing each time.

Shane had some things he needed to do and was unable to stay all night, so I called my friend Joyce. She came and spent all night in the recliner, witnessing the fact that they refused to check my heel as I complained about the pain. She commented about how absurd the idea was. I was tremendously disappointed because this put an end to my walking dreams for now. I remember wanting to get the opportunity to walk so badly that I only looked forward to returning to Health South for one more chance, even if it meant crying myself to sleep without morphine.

I still continue to work my right arm so that the left might be able to imitate it and relearn the movement, but nothing happened. I still want to believe that Eugene will work again because I know that God can reconnect those nerves to my brain any time He wants to, but once again, it is difficult when confronted with the deadness every day.

Finally, after a week, they told me I would be moved back to rehab once again where I could get back into therapy. I was very excited because I remembered the wound nurse who had attended to me before when I was there, and I was confident that she would fix my heel. The day I checked in to rehab a week after my trip to the ER, I remember it was the smallest room I had ever seen, and it was a different floor than I was on before. Therefore, I had all new nurses and many new techs.

I requested that the wound specialist, Sunday, look at my heel, but Sunday was off work. So no one really paid any attention to my complaints about it hurting. It is a slow process of building strength in the right side while teaching the left side all of the things it used to do naturally. It was not going well for me as my heel was hurting more and more and inhibiting me from making real progress in PT. Working with my arm and learning how to master simple daily activities seemed near impossible, but I struggled every day to prove I could do it. I never dreamed it could be this difficult to brush my teeth.

My mom was there, either in person or on the phone, checking on me and constantly reminding me of the horrible situation I was in. She never meant to bring pain; however, she just didn't understand the emotional pain that losing a limb could evoke and how difficult it was to regain control of my mind with it all. Every time she would ask how I was, I wanted to burst into tears because I could not even think of any words that would describe my sorrow. I knew that our minds control our bodies, but when it no longer comes naturally, it is the strangest thing. I had no true understanding, yet I expected someone to understand and try to comfort me.

After weeks of therapy, I was moved to my cousin's rental home; it was a one-story building, so I could wheel around in more easily. My sister, Valerie, was living with my mom only a few blocks away, so when Mike was at work and Shane was not able to be there, my sister would come help out. I remember I still had no muscle control on my stub side, so it was difficult but very necessary to keep my stub from going into the toilet as I was sat on the toilet seat. My sister was the first to dunk it in the toilet, and boy, did we get a great laugh.

I really needed to laugh about something, and this was about to be one of the funniest days that we experienced. Valerie had taken me to the bathroom that time, and while standing me up to pull my pants up, she had back pain and dropped me on the cold tile floor. I got my good leg up under me enough to help push as she pulled, but we were both laughing so hard that I was sliding back toward the floor. She tried again to no avail, and I got as comfortable as possible to wait until she got help, knowing that together we were not going to get me back in that chair. As Val went to the living room to size up our options, I realized that my panties were around my ankles, my female existence exposed to anyone who might enter. Just as she entered the room, she saw my brother in-law pull in the driveway; and thinking this was the answer, she came back into the bathroom to tell me. I looked down as I lie on the floor all spread out and exposed and told her that David, my brother-in-law, would not want to help us under the circumstances.

It wasn't long before she came back in to tell me about a high school girlfriend that was jogging by and had stopped to talk to Dave. She asked if she should ask her to help us. I probably blushed thinking about seeing an old and not very familiar friend in this condition. We decided to wait for Mike to get home from work because it wouldn't be much longer, and I was being well stretched in this new position. Mike came in, and I heard Val explaining what had happened to him in the other room. In order to speed things along, I yelled his name, and he could not help but laugh when he saw me there. He got me up very easily, and all was well unlike that time weeks later when I fell in the kitchen floor and broke my shoulder, adding another specialist to my long list of doctors. I had a hard time finding many laughable moments, but Val always seemed to bring them out in me. A good belly laugh is good for the health, so I surely got one that day.

When I had my prosthetic leg, I had to forget everything I had learned my whole life and learn a whole new process of walking. There was always so much to do and so little improvement that I was discouraged often. I always felt like I would take two steps forward and then three backward. The top of it was made of fiberglass, and I was so disappointed at how heavy it was and difficult to get on. I struggled to do what they told me to do but never felt comfortable with it no matter how the therapists praised me. Because I only had use of one arm, it will always be more difficult for me than for some, but that only fuels my fire to complete rehab.

I know that in every rehab facility I have been in, they have given me psychological testing to determine that I had no serious brain damage from this ordeal, but there are times that I cannot put together a complete thought or remember the simplest things. My boys poke fun about my stupidity often, and I try to ignore them, even though I question it sometimes, understanding why my family does not trust most of what I say. I always feel like they question or write off everything that I say, leaving me desperate for real communication.

In November, I was released from the rehab with a huge sore on my left heel that I will always believe was a result of neglect and nonaggressive treatment. I was told to locate a wound clinic and visit them as soon as possible, which I did. Everyone was telling me that the wound should be scraped. But when the nurse there, after looking at it, said, "I can't scrape this, but I will slice some lines into the sore to promote healing."

She used a scalpel and cut vertical and horizontal lines into the sore, almost bringing me off the table several times in my pain. I was never seen by a physician either of the two times I visited this office. Once again, I trusted in what they were doing, as my sore became bigger and greener. This clinic advised that I go to a vascular specialist at this point, and of course, I followed direction. He convinced me and my son that my circulation was so poor I would need an angioplasty in both legs, so we started with the left leg. The angioplasty was scheduled, once again, to promote healing.

After a rough two years, I was willing to do whatever they told me, believing that they knew the answers and could make it better. I left there with a Band-Aid and directions to continue cleaning and applying Santyle ointment, which had done nothing to promote any healing. We made it through yet another disappointing doctor's visit, with no relief from the pain. I was losing faith in the entire medical profession, learning that the Santyle ointment was a debridement and should have only been used in the beginning of the pressure sore and not continually as prescribed. I wished I had a wound specialist in the family. My heel was very painful, so I continued to wear my bubble boot every night since I left the rehab hospital even though my heel continued to rot.

Since the medical profession continued to fail me again and again, I looked online and to friends to find a remedy, but nothing made sense except to keep it clean, which we did. Simple Clean and Santyle were prescribed, so that's what we continued to use. I wish I could have those days back so badly, just another reason to live every day to its fullest, leaving no room for regret. It was too late for me, and I had so many regrets by this time.

The hardest thing was to trust this new leg to hold me as my old one had. I have balanced checkbooks and balanced being a mother, a pastor's wife, and teaching young people all at the same time—but this was a whole new balancing act, and I often doubted that I could ever do it. Balance did not come easy, but it was going to come. So I had to keep believing and be patient. I certainly heard that a lot. I seemed to be the only one who knew I would have to have a different kind of leg if I was ever going to walk. They all continued to praise me while I knew that I was wasting time conquering a leg that would never be an extension of me. I was very depressed about the whole leg situation and wished I was an engineer and could design my own.

14

The Apartment at the End of the Hall

Because I always had so many people with me and Shane stayed all night, they asked if I would be interested in moving to the training apartment at the end of the hall. It was a huge room that we all checked out every morning on the way to breakfast. We envied whoever lived in there as it was such a big space.

I later learned that this was a rehab training apartment that was used to get patients to be able to transition for going home. It was glorious and just in time. My mom arrived and of course wanted to take care of everything like moms do. She began asking about my heel as well, but nothing intentional was done to treat it. Shane began to question why they were not medicating my heel with something, but still nothing no one did something about it.

I later found a tube of pink medication on my bedside table, and when I questioned why it was not used, it was explained to me that bedsores were different; they had to heal from the inside out, and this medication called Calmoseptine was not going to help it. It was made to be used at a different stage of the sore. I later learned that this was exactly what my sore needed because I got another pressure sore on my chest, and I immediately applied this ointment and my sore dried up in two weeks. But it sat on my bedside table, never applied. To learn this many months later made me feel so cheated by the medical institution that I had trusted, knowing that all of what was about to come could have all been prevented.

They ordered me a boot to sleep in at night and always had it raised off the bed, but still no medication was applied. They ordered me a motion bed that would roll, trying to prevent any more bedsores. Their preventative efforts were commendable, but they should have sent me back to the hospital to treat my heel. They knew that my heel should not be in this shape, and they did not know what to do about it.

I continued to do therapy each day as it became more and more uncomfortable to wear my leg brace because it rubbed my sore. They took care of that by sending the brace back to have a hole cut in the heel so the sore would be surrounded by the brace instead of on top of it. It still rubbed. One night, as my mom lay in the bed beside me, I noticed that my heel was oozing, and I assumed that it might be stuck to my sock.

The tech that came in to give me a bath was someone I had never had before. She undressed me for the shower. Then she took the toe of my no-skid sock and yanked it off, exposing my heel and shooting blood all over my room. My mother jumped up and was very agitated that after all this time, my heel had been exposed this way. I immediately requested that Sunday be called but was told that she had left for the day.

I made a formal report against this tech because of her attitude and treatment of the situation, and the following day, the floor nurse interviewed me about the situation. There were still no aggressive healing attempts toward my heel. The following morning, however, Sunday appeared and began photographing my heel and cleaning it and applying a protective coating that was in a package like the alcohol pad. Finally, someone was concerned about my heel besides me and my family.

The medical physician still had not seen my heel. However, his assistant would stop by at breakfast and ask how I was doing. My heel became more and more painful every day, but there was no helpful treatment being done, and I was never made aware of how serious this matter could be. I was confused as to why they did not send me back to the hospital if they were unable to relieve me of my problem, but no one had any answers except for a few nurses who told me that they had seen bed sores that were so big they could get their fist inside it, making me feel like I had nothing to complain about since at that time, my sore was the size of a dime on my heel.

They knew that my heel should not be in this shape, and they did not know what to do about it. I was caught in the middle of a horrible place, wanting to walk so badly but thinking that it couldn't be good for my foot because of the pain it caused. "No pain, no gain" became a reality instead of a motivational statement. My heel was in pain all the time. I definitely experienced malpractice or medical neglect, but I had grown to love this place that had become my home away from home, so I never discussed it.

Shane continued to question what we could do about it and suggested draining the blood and allowing air to get to it to dry it up, but they seemed irritated that he could possibly know more about this, and they always made us feel stupid because we did not understand the difference of treating a bed sore. Possibly if we had treated this as a plain sore, it would have gone away. My biggest regret is that I did not demand that they do something more for my heel or at the very least send me back to the hospital where it all began. It was so complicated, yet I had faith that the wound specialist was going to fix this, so I endured the pain, continued to learn to walk, and allowed the abuse, which was exactly what it was by this time.

Eugene had no voluntary movement at all, and everyone but Shane and I had given up on the possibility that it ever would. But since I knew how important it was to my overall health, I had to keep believing. I continued awakening my facial muscles. The brace they had made for my leg was rubbing my heel so badly that they sent it out to have the heel cut out of it, so I was usually in tears as I accomplished my therapy. Finally, Tammy told me that I did not need to do any more because the shoe was rubbing my sore so badly. I felt like I was forced to give up physical therapy, therefore putting my dream out of reach again.

After being released from rehab a second time, we were instructed to go to a wound clinic as soon as possible. I was not given any reference or my records, but I was on my own now to fix what they had neglected for so long. Money was tight due to so many medical expenses, but I still had enough therapy visits to do some outpatient therapy back at rehab. I was told that outpatient rehab would be covered, unaware that I had a ten thousand dollar deductible that I had not met, making this some pretty expensive therapy.

I worked with new therapists but loved going and getting the work out just the same. My OT was awesome and she got Eugene to move more than ever before through E-stim, electrical stimulation. I believe that if I had been given that earlier my hand would have made a recovery, but I'm not a Doctor. (**thanks, Chelsae**). I soon used up all the visits that Insurance would allow so it was back to Shane and I trying to work through the pain and walk the driveway.

At this time, we spent all our days traveling to doctors' offices and discovering wound clinics and specialists that might be able to help with my heel. No one really did anything to help. We felt very alone in our quest to conquer this sore, only cleaning it with the Santyle ointment that they supplied from rehab. I felt so cheated, knowing that if I was rich, I would have been treated differently and would have walked out of therapy a healed woman instead of unfixable like I felt at my release. I experienced discrimination as well as malpractice, and I knew it but could not get anyone to care or listen.

Many months of extreme pain followed. I remember a time when we were on our way out to dinner with our best friends. I looked at my husband in the eye, tears threatening to flow, and asked, "Am I going to lose my foot?"

He responded, as he always did, "No, you'll be fine."

Boy was he wrong on this one. I never really believed that I was in jeopardy of losing my foot, but I have always been aware of the risk because of my diabetes, leading me to take good care of my feet.

Mike was tired and overworked and so badly in need of help with all the changes my health had placed in our lives that he decided we would move back to Kentucky so that my mom might be able to help us. Due to my health and the fact that my family was so spread out and the medical bills were taking over our lives, we thought that it would be best living in my mom's house for a short time, then moving to my grandmother's house so that we may be able to pay off some bills by living there.

My cousin bought my Nan-naws house and agreed to rent it to us, so we moved there. My grandmother had passed away, and no one was living in her house, so I thought that we may be able to pay off some bills by living there. Mike was so overwhelmed taking on all my responsibilities plus working full time just to keep the insurance and pay the medical bills. So the decision was made in order to be near family, we would move back to Kentucky.

While still in outpatient therapy at Health South, I began to investigate therapy opportunities in Louisville before we actually moved. Frazier Rehab was highly recommended, and I began rehab three times a week once we moved to Louisville. On my second visit to physical therapy, my therapist wanted to look at my heel. As she took the bandage off, she called for their nurse to come and look at it. The two of them discussed privately and advised me to go to the ER immediately.

My family seemed to blame Mike in a lot of ways for our position and were not as supportive of him as I wanted them to be. No one ever recognized the importance of talking to him or giving him an outlet to vent about what all had happened to us. This had not just affected me but my entire family, especially Mike. My mom would come by daily to check on me, but since I had to still be taken to the restroom and to and from my chair, and her health was so bad, she could not be of much assistance to me or my husband. My sister was available but didn't help except with the physical lifting because she has her own issues and really can't. So we moved a great distance for very little help or reason as Mike found himself looking for another job.

15

A Knub?

On top of everything else I now began to worry about losing a foot that I had worked so hard to rehabilitate. Mike was tired and overworked and so badly in need of help with all of the changes my health had placed in our lives that he decided we would move back to Kentucky, so that my mom might be able to help us. Due to my health and the fact that my family was so spread out and the medical bills were taking over our lives, we thought that it would be best living in my mom's house for a short time then moving to my grandmother's house so that we may be able to pay off some bills by living there. My cousin bought my Nan-naws house and agreed to rent it to us so we moved. forgetting that my mother was eighty years old and having knee surgery. My grandmother had passed away and no one was living in her house so I thought that we may be able to pay off some bills by living there. Mike was so overwhelmed taking on all of my responsibilities plus working full time just to keep insurance and drowning in medical bills, so the decision was made in order to be near family, we would move back to Kentucky. While still in outpatient therapy at Health South, Huntsville Alabama, I began to investigate therapy opportunities in Louisville before we actually moved. Frazier Rehab was highly recommended and I began rehab 3 times a week, once we moved to Louisville.

On my second visit to PT, my therapist wanted to look at my heel and as she took the bandage off she called for their nurse to come and look at it. They discussed me privately then both advised me to go to ER immediately.

My son took me to ER at Baptist East Hospital. The medics immediately called the specialist, the best amputee surgeon in the country. My family was there as Dr. Bergamini told me that it was too far gone and he did not think that just taking the foot would help me that he would have to go above the knee. I heard the words but had no idea what was truly being said. He convinced me and my family that due to the amount of infection and the weakness of my heart, I should have the surgery the next morning at 11:00.

The only question I had was, "Would I ever be able to walk again on this foot?" He told me that not only would I never walk but the infection would move to my heart and take my life if this amputation did not happen immediately.

Here we go again. How can God allow this to happen to me? I questioned everything that I knew about God, and I could not see Him wanting this for me. Quickly I was reminded that I was strong enough to get beyond all of this because God knew this even when I was blinded by all my pain. The time frame seemed to be so quick that I hardly had time to pray about what was coming next. But it came just the same. I had truly experienced more pain and for a longer time than anything I had ever been through before. I had a few fleeting moments of peace as I looked in the eyes of all my family, and I was ready, ready to hear the details of a horrifying surgery, which I have second-guessed many times since then, wondering if God wanted me to just trust Him to heal the infection.

The doctor went on to say, "Because your heart was so weak, we are unable to knock you out completely due to the risk it would put on your heart." He said it would be a twilight sleep, assuring me that I would not feel it but that I may experience some sounds due to the fact that they use a saw to cut through the bone as the surgery progressed.

I was totally unprepared for what was about to happen. Memories of all the dances we had attended and the amount of exercise that I enjoyed so much came flooding back and filled my mind with sorrow. I may never have another chance to add to those special memories.

The day after my amputation, I remember a nurse getting me to sign a paper stating it was all right for my leg to travel to a funeral home to be incinerated. I don't know why, but signing this made me a little sick to my stomach. I looked as though I had fallen down and skinned my knee, although this time, I no longer had a knee. I know that I had many family members that would have changed places with me if it were possible; however, when I think about that, I know that I am the right one. I praise God that He trusts me enough to get through this because I will get through this, and we will all come out on the other side in His grace. I knew that I would do it if only I could trust Him enough to help me.

At this time, I had no idea of the difficulties that would come. I had never known anyone with a prosthetic and did not understand how it would all work, even though I knew it could, I took no comfort in that. After losing my leg, mourning set in. The truth hit me: I no longer would ever have a leg again. I would forever be dependent on someone for help. I had that leg for fifty-five years.

I tried so hard to be strong for my friends and family. My family has seen me as a faithful cornerstone with a great relationship with Christ, and now the test had come. I believe God was giving me a chance to show everyone that dependency on Him is the only way to rejoice in such a sad, difficult time. And I was not doing so well. I dealt with a lot of phantom pains; meaning, my leg still hurt as though it was still there. It would even itch at times with nothing there to scratch.

I was afraid to tell anyone how I was feeling for fear they would prescribe another medication to the list I was already uncomfortably taking. I learned to hide my pain and disappointment well. I also had to deal with my anger as I blamed this hospital and rehab facility for my loss. The Lord was teaching me again a lesson about how treacherous anger can be. I was so angry at health south for not caring for this bed sore while I was there, I had to learn how to embrace forgiveness for this hospital.

I could not see the incision on my leg, but once the bandages came off, I could feel the cut. It was a horizontal slit across the bottom of where my knee had been, creating loose skin on both sides that fell toward the floor. My boys had a laugh at it as it looked like a butt crack. We have had many laughs over my second butt crack.

Next, I was introduced to a small stocking called a shrinker that was supposed to form my knub to fit into a prosthetic. To be honest, it sounded very painful at first. Just thinking about putting my stub down into a fiberglass shell and putting weight on it made me have mixed feelings. I was looking forward to walking but wished I could skip the pain leading up to it. I was overjoyed about possibly walking again. But I feared the process, and I was unaware of what all it entailed. The surgery that I was promised would end my pain only offered me a whole new pain, one that I could not see beyond.

The next day came, and my stub hurt. But I was told that it looked wonderful; the incision was a beautiful job well done. I could have cared less, but a good job meant less chance of infection or a corrective surgery of any kind, so that sounded good to me. I did not remember any sawing sounds, but I did faintly hear some sounds and especially voices throughout the surgery, but thanks to drugs and the sacrifice of my limb, I felt no more pain in my heel.

I remember crying to Mike that I was so tired of pain and that all I wanted was for it to end. I did not realize it then, but my pain was causing Mike much pain as well. He wanted to help me so badly but could do nothing. It wasn't very long until a prosthetist—I had no idea what a prosthetist was until this day, but it didn't sound like anything a good Christian should be doing—came. After an introduction with him, he casted me for a prosthetic, making things much clearer, and informing me that I would be getting a new leg soon.

I was released from the hospital very quickly and shifted to another rehab facility to learn to use my new leg.

I had two young very sweet nephews who call me Aunt Sissy (because their dad, my brother, calls me Sissy). I enjoyed watching play their sports. Every opportunity I got, I was at a football, soccer, or basketball game cheering them on. I couldn't wait to get out so I could continue to watch each season. When I got sick, they visited me often with my brother, Chad. Charlie, ten years old, would ask appropriate questions about my leg and would always make a special effort to tell me he loved me before leaving each night. The little things that mean so much. Hearing those words would bring tears to my eyes.

Several evenings, their whole family visited. They once brought a spaghetti dinner for us all. I had not gotten to know my brother's new wife, Nicole, very well, but I gratefully saw a side of her that I never saw in my brother's first wife. I loved her then and there. I can remember feeling normal for the first time in a very long time as we all sat in the kitchen area and ate together. I needed normal, so I looked forward to those visits. The boys would beat me at Farkle, a game of numbers, and I was always amazed at how smart they were. I would lose gracefully. Then when it's time for them to go home, I would await Charlie's, "Good night. I love you, Aunt Sissy." It always gives me happy thoughts to ponder as I go to bed.

I had not taken any pain meds for three days, so I was proud of myself and hopeful that I might break the ugly cycle. I have always hated drugs, fearful of any long-term effects that I may not be educated about.

My mother in-law was in a nursing home in Louisville, so my father in-law and Mike's brother, Dave, would come by my place every evening on their way to see her. I was always blessed with company. I teased them because they always came around dinnertime and helped me finish my meals, saying that the food was good, and I was grateful somebody liked it. One evening, my good friends Keith and Dee brought Kentucky Fried Chicken, and we all had a picnic outside, once again making me believe in the idea of normal for myself again.

I later learned that the biggest injustice in all of this is that the lawyers in Huntsville would not give me any attention because there was not enough money in it for them to take on an institution like this hospital. At that point, I had given up faith in the medical and law profession. I watched every crime show while hospitalized, and all the criminals had to do was say, "I want a lawyer," and one would appear. I called every lawyer in Huntsville, seeking justice, but I was turned down. The last lawyer I spoke to said that it would have to go to a jury trial, and it would take too much money to make it worth it. I knew that I had been a victim of neglect, and it saddened me that our judicial system allowed a woman who spilled hot coffee on herself to win a lawsuit against McDonald's but I couldn't get anyone to listen to me when nothing that happened to me was fault.

I have to move beyond this and am continuing to give it my all; however, it would be easier if someone would step up to try to make any of this right. I had moved twice, so my husband was emailing lawyers all over the country, but it seems that Alabama is protected in that it has to be a state-certified attorney. My husband contacted yet another lawyer who works in Alabama, and I too emailed her a request for assistance, therefore we are waiting another response, probably a rejection letter.

I chose to make a call to the head doctor at the rehabilitation hospital, and he acted surprised that I had any issues with his care. He shared that he had already spoken to my husband, and he thought it was the fault of the hospital and not the rehab center. He was nice enough to speak with me, but still he left me with so many unanswered questions. I had no real closure. I was awaiting a response from another malpractice firm at that time, so I was careful as to what I said. Two days later, I received a call from the CEO of the rehab center. He asked me if it would help if he arranged a conference call between himself, the doctor, the wound specialist, and myself. I agreed that it would help me a great deal, so he scheduled a conference call.

Meanwhile the attorney's office called me, so I asked them the morning of the scheduled call and I asked if it would be all right and they advised me not to answer the call at all and just let it ring. As difficult as it was, I allowed the phone to ring three different times without answering. I felt even more troubled that I had now wasted an important man's time, and I wished I had responded to his attempt to offer me some peace.

My husband wanted a huge lawsuit because we were near bank-ruptcy, and this was all because of their negligence. He knew that there would continue to be medical bills throughout my future due to this loss, and he had watched me suffer with extraordinary pain for a very long time. My pain was his pain, and he believed they owed me a substantial monetary amount; at least some assistance with the medical bills we owed them would have been nice. He wanted some-one to talk to us about what we were entitled to, if anything.

16

Bradenton

We moved to Florida because it's warm and sunny and in order to have the opportunity to practice walking every day. Since my dad and Nan lived in Bradenton, Mike took a job near the area hoping for some help. Mike gets up every morning at five, which works well for me because I always had to pee by then. He delivers tires all day, all over the areas around Tampa, and gets home around six in the evenings, leaving Shane or Jared to care for me every day.

Setting up new doctors and adapting to their new opinions was difficult to adjust to. For instance, my cardiologist couldn't believe that I had not been given a defibrillator; he recommended that I get one instantly. I began testing for one and tried to get insurance to agree to pay. I had requested my medical records and filled out medical authorization for release forms on several occasions, but still without records. It had been four long months of waiting and calling my cardiologist's office daily until I finally got the procedure scheduled. I was told it could be soon.

I did get a new prosthetist, and he created a new leg for me. It is easier for me to get it on, but still, it's nowhere easy as it looks on TV. My new leg is covered in U of K print, one of my sons' early pillowcases, since my family were all big fans of Kentucky basketball.

I'll never have to tell anyone which college team I pulled for, and I knew that my nephews would love it. I practiced walking, building muscles. I continued to need prayer, friends, and support more than anything else.

We live in a small apartment, so for the first time ever, my wants are overshadowing my needs. My biggest want is a way to make this all work without me being a burden to somebody. Independence is something that each American takes for granted, and it makes me sad to revisit how I thought before these last few months occurred.

I was so certain that I was neglected in my medical treatment that I continued to contact malpractice attorneys, only to be told that without my medical records, they could not help me. I was angry and had lost any respect for the law at this point, but I continued to request for my records. The rehab center gave me a plastic folder upon discharge with the CEO's card tucked in a slot in the front. I then called his cell number daily, requesting and then demanding my records. Of course, he would have his kindhearted secretary call me back the following day, but at least, I was able to talk to someone. She informed me that they sent their files to a holding company, so I called them and developed a relationship with the director of medical records, once again filling out the same authorization papers as before. I continued to call my CEO friend, wanting so badly for someone to understand how necessary these records were to my decisions regarding my future health, and I was now in this for the long haul.

Finally, the secretary assured me that she was sending my records certified mail on Monday, so I patiently waited for the mailman to knock on my door as I sat beside it in my lift chair. The week came to an end and still nothing. So I called the secretary every day. The Wednesday of the following week, I received a pick up notice in our mailbox and instantly got my daughter, who was visiting, to take me to the post office to retrieve them. I wanted so bad to read the recorded facts about what had happened in my lack of medical treatment that led to this bed sore.

Since it took much longer to have me out of the car and into my wheelchair, Taylor asked if she could just run in and fetch it for me.

As she shut the car door, I allowed my mind to wander. What might be in these records, and how would the photos they had taken each day might better tell the story? She was gone about three minutes with an envelope that I knew could not possibly hold eight months of medical records. My heart sank.

She got into the car, announcing that she did not think this was what I had been waiting for; and sure enough, as she opened the envelope and pulled out two sheets of paper, I felt sick: two more authorization for medical release forms, the third one was I had filled out. Anger and disappointment once again. I had been patiently awaiting these all-too-familiar results. Something had to change.

I immediately called the useless CEO, telling him that I could now relate to why people storm into places of business and begin shooting at people. I realized much later how threatening I sounded and wondered if the police might show up at some point that evening. I meant it though. I knew it, and even worse, he knew that they had purposefully held my records beyond the two-year litigation period, knowing that I could do nothing about the unprofessional treatment I received at his hospital. I was pissed (as my sister would say), a word that I never use; however, it was suitable in this situation.

I began to think more and more about writing as I was encouraged by many to write a book. I began to pray about it and was assured that if my story could encourage just one person and they could see how my relationship with Jesus got me through, then I should write it all down. *This Book* began in tragedy will end in triumph. Writing in itself became an important therapy for me as well, and I believe it helped me recapture so many memories. This was something for me to do that only I could, and I vowed to follow through with this no matter how long it took me. I'm not sure how to write a book, especially when I feel like it has not ended yet, but I'm giving it my best effort, so keep reading. I know that God Himself inspired me to write, and He who began a good work in you is faithful to complete it (Rom. 8:28). Praise God.

The first thing we set out to find when we arrive in Bradenton was a ministry to fill the void we felt from not being in service to our Lord. We struggled to find a Bible-preaching church in our small town. Finally deciding on a community church out of desperation, we settled, even though we knew we would not get the expository preaching we desired. We committed to an off-campus small group and planned to attend a study about being a real Christian. After all we had been through, we desperately needed some Christian friends in this new town, so we were happy to attend.

On the day of the study, I received a dismissal letter from my cardiologist, who actually called me combative and belligerent, stating this as the reason he would no longer treat me. He gave me thirty days to find a new doctor. I kept all my disgust inside, not responding to his letter, except with prayer. The next letter I opened was another refusal to take our malpractice case against my health provider. I was discouraged to say the least as we headed out to find this study group. As we discussed a book by Todd Wilson called *Real Christian*, I was under such conviction as we talked about a statement he made regarding forgiveness. It said, "A lamblike disposition… This, biblically speaking, is not optional. Forgiving others is one of the defining marks of a real Christian." I knew that God was speaking directly to me and several of my circumstances that had occurred this very day. I was so grateful to know exactly what to do with all of this and looked forward to having the freedom to move forward.

Since moving to Florida, my son was working nights at the local paper for very little money and was unhappy at work. He had to sleep all day so he could have the energy to return another night. I was surprised when he talked to me about joining the armed forces. I instantly knew that it would be a great answer for him to have the successful life that he deserved. He began to take steps to make it come about. His biggest concern as always was me and who would care for me. But it looked like Jared would be here when Shane had to leave, so we were all preparing for his day at the end of November. I am so grateful for his service. May God richly bless Shane for all of his sacrifices for me, and may God enable me to achieve a point where I will never again need anyone the way I have needed him.

God is putting all the pieces in place, and I thank God that I can see that now and will be pliable as He continues to work in our entire family.

The army quickly got Shane set up, and he received a date to be shipped out. I could feel his excitement build each day as the time drew near. He needed to live a life of his own, and I need to relearn how to depend on God, myself, and Mike from then on. I know that all of the previous two years has prepared him for something very special, and I know that it won't take the Armed Forces long to realize what an asset he is to their branch of service. I am assured that God has big plans for him. I will await another graduation date, a new life to unfold, and who knows, maybe some grandkids?

I was so happy for him, but I was a little frightened to do life for the first time in two years without him. We began to make other plans about what to do with me, and it worked out that indeed my oldest son would be returning home in time to take over. God is so good, even in the smallest details, and I love the plan. My beautiful daughter calls often and reads God's word with me on FaceTime. She read me Job, and it reminded me that he too struggled and approached the Lord about his pain. I was very encouraged, and I appreciated Taylor taking me to the word.

I was getting stronger both physically, mentally, and emotionally. I could even talk about my struggles without sobbing. I think I could maybe talk about it in the form of testimony someday without bawling my eyes out. My dream would be to revisit a couple of the churches from my past that have literally prayed for me through this and be able to give testimony about how good God has been in spite of me and my questions and doubt. I truly believe that God will also give me that opportunity somewhere in my future, but until then, I will continue to trust God, knowing He has a plan and believing whole heartily that *This Book* is a part of it.

As hard as I fight back the tears, they still come. As Washington Irving once said, "There is a sacredness in tears. They are not a sign of weakness, but of power. They speak more eloquently than ten thousand tongues. They are the messengers of overwhelming grief, of deep contrition and of unspeakable love."

17

What? A Defibrillator?

When I first visited my new cardiologist, he was surprised that no one had given me a defibrillator, and he wanted me to consider one immediately. He convinced me that I may not live to even see the surgery without wearing a vest that would shock my heart back into rhythm if it should try to shut off before I could get the defibrillator installed. So I had people come to my house and hook me up to a vest.

I wore the vest one day thinking it was too uncomfortable. The leads were irritating my back, and I was fearful of getting another bedsore. The procedure was scheduled for July 22, but my insurance company would not pay for it, claiming it was a new procedure and mechanism; therefore, three appeals were made by my doctor and myself. They declined it again, so for my wellbeing, the doctor said we should go ahead with a regular defibrillator attached to my heart. So I looked forward to Medicare while awaiting this next procedure, something that would automatically shock me if my heart stopped pumping or got in an irregular rhythm.

I once again bought into this suggestion for fear of not seeing grandkids and missing out on so much of my children's lives. I had to completely trust this medically respected doctor. He described that I would have an evasive machine put under my arm and that even though it was a newer procedure, it would be the safest for my situation. My doctor scheduled the date of the surgery with the hospital, but he referred me to another doctor for the actual procedure since he did not perform the actual surgery. I informed my family of this new procedure, and my daughter planned a flight to Florida to be with me.

Then I received a call from my cardiologist's office, informing me that insurance was denying the procedure. I spent many hours toggling back and forth between offices as to what the next step would be. The surgeon told me that he was going to make a physician appeal to my insurance company, and they informed me that I could also repeal their denial, which I did. I was on the phone many times every day, trying to get this all set up and getting the doctors, insurance company, and the hospital all on the same page.

I then received a call from the hospital requiring more testing. They informed me that the procedure had been approved. My daughter had returned to her home, but I assured her that this was a minor outpatient procedure, so all was well After a couple of days, I learned that the call from the hospital was a mistake, and we still had no approval. So I recalled both offices trying to figure out what exactly was going on. But I was told that they had appealed it several times; they recommended that I just have the regular evasive defibrillator that is implanted above the heart and has a small lead going into my heart. I agreed just to get this all behind me, so for the third time a surgery date was given. Of course, the blood work had to be redone since so much time had elapsed.

They tried to make it all very easy on me, knowing the struggle I was having, so they scheduled the tests the same morning of the procedure, allowing me to check in to the hospital one time and get it all accomplished. I had the procedure before lunch, and everything went well. The hospital charged my insurance company $63,000 for this minor surgery, only adding to my already overwhelming medical debt.

I had to spend the night in the hospital on my thirty-fourth wedding anniversary, with Shane still by my side, wanting to get home as soon as possible. My doctor was out of town, so his partner visited me the next morning and released me, saying, "You will need to follow up with your cardiologist next week. Make sure that the stitches do not bleed, and keep it dry." I left the hospital with a patch on my chest.

Six days after my procedure, my husband and I were sitting at a red light and were hit from behind, thrusting me forward and causing some fresh blood on my patch. Luck doesn't appear to be on my side, so I guess it's a good thing I do not believe in it. I immediately called my doctor, informing him that I was going to have the staples removed the next day. He advised me to just wait and let them take care of it. As I entered my cardiologist's office, I told him about the wreck. He lifted the corner of the bandage and said that we needed to wait another week to take the stitches out, so another appointment was made. He went on to say that the bandage I had put on it was better than anything he had in his office, so he tried to re-stick my bloody bandage down.

When my husband came home from work, he so upset seeing the dirty bandage that he called the doctor's office and told the secretary that I lost my leg because of medical negligence, so he was going to be more cautious. He questioned why they would allow me to leave the office in a bloody bandage to which they had no answers. It was a bad position to be in when you are so dependent on the medical professionals for your life that you really aren't afforded an opinion or thought.

We were all frustrated because of what happened, and the same sick feeling came upon me once again, keeping me awake yet another night. I tried to remain unbothered, knowing that I wanted these staples to come out as soon as possible and that I had to return to the clinic for that to happen. I had zero control of my life, my health, or my pain. Tylenol was the only pain medication I was allowed. The uncertainties of my life were getting the best of me as I tried my best to continue to hide my disappointments from everyone in my life. We had no church. No permanent promise of housing. No good credit. No local friends. No real plan other than trusting God for each step, which I was very uncertain I could take. The times were not getting more promising for us, and depression was becoming harder and harder for me to overcome.

The next day, the mailman informed me that I got a certified letter in the mail. It was from my heart doctor. He informed me that he could no longer act as my cardiologist, and like an arrogant unprofessional, he called me belligerent and combative. I then had thirty days to find a new doctor who would accept my insurance They are all practicing medicine, and in my situation, practice should have been called off long before my leg was taken.

I am and will forever be at the mercy of the medical profession and my insurance company, and that is not a comfortable place when you have the kind of problems that I have. Trusting God is one thing, but when you have to trust doctors, it is a whole new game, a difficult one to figure out because insurance and the medical offices do not work together for our good. They make it nearly impossible for us to get the needed treatment, and it angers me after all we have gone through.

Once again, I am thankful that I don't have to trust in anything in this world. I look forward to the world that I am promised by God, one of happiness and glory, where there will be no pain and no suffering. The only way to look forward to such a place is to know the Savior that offered His life that it might be possible for us after we leave this world. Please do not delay, Lord, as I look forward to heavenly days. If you know Him and know someone who doesn't, now is the perfect time to discuss what the Bible says about where you will each spend eternity. That's a long time to be on the wrong side of an easy decision. My strongest prayer through the writing of this book is that someone who reads it might lead someone else to make an eternal decision because of something they have read. If you are one of those, I praise God for making all of this possible, and I thank you for your obedience to be all you can be for His glory.

As I pondered why all of these horrible medical issues kept complicating our lives and never going according to plan, I was reminded by Mike that Mary had no intension of having her firstborn baby in a manger in a strange town. What thoughts must have passed through her young, inexperienced mind? She wasn't looking for a miracle;

however, she knew the Lord well enough to call on Him by name. I also know Him and will continue to depend on Him and call His name.

I still find it so hard to believe that what started as a small pressure sore has ended in a life-changing event that has messed with every aspect of my life. What's more was that no one really wanted to care, hear, or take responsibility for what they have done to me. Lawyers say it is the diabetes and the fact that I have no medical records. My Christian friends and family say it's God's will. My son says it's my opportunity to prove the power of God to many through witnessing my journey. I just want closure so that I can get beyond the pity, motionlessness, excessive use of the restroom, and lack of exercise.

This is yet another opportunity to reach my goal of independence. Thank you to so many who have prayed this for me. I will no longer let any of you down as I will walk again with the Lord's help and strong arm. Although I am still praying for independence however God chooses to accomplish it, I try to practice with my prosthesis every day, and I certainly have hope that I can learn to maneuver like those seen on TV. I am finally content to accept whatever God wants to do with me or for me. I will prevail because He has already won the war so that I can win the battle. No matter how bad it looks to me, it looks like an amazing opportunity to Him, and that is what matters. I pray I can focus on what matters for the remainder of my time here. I still hold onto the hope that Eugene would be able to raise above my head one day and really praise the Lord.

18

The Visit

Shane had a roommate in college who played on the basketball team. He is Mattie from Australia, with the full Aussie accent, and almost seven feet tall. Shane had the opportunity to visit with his amazing family for a month at Christmas, having an unbelievable time touring his wonderful country. Matt had visited with us for a few weeks earlier, but we lived in Alabama at the time. He was at the hospital with Shane and Taylor when I awoke from my open-heart surgery in 2011 as well. He is such a great young man and a dear friend to my son.

While sitting at home doing very little, Shane told me that Mattie is coming to the United States for a visit, but it's supposed to be a surprise, so I had to act like I don't know. He was flying in to New Orleans and had so many people to visit en route to see us.

Shane was not sure when Mattie would actually arrive due to the number of stops he planned to make along the way. Mattie did not have a cell phone, so he would stop and use free Wi-Fi and message Shane along the way. We had gone to a doctor's appointment. When we were returning home, Shane said, "Matt should be here around five o'clock tonight." Sure enough, he came in shortly after five. It was so awesome to see him and entertaining to hear about his tales of getting here.

A new movie called *The Visit* had just come to theaters, and a commercial had been airing for weeks that petrified me. The story goes that some kids went to visit their grandparents for a break that turned deadly. It scared me every time I saw this ad and I couldn't imagine why anyone would want to see it. When Matt was waiting to meet up with a friend in Alabama, he had nothing to do, so he drove to the movies. The only movie available at the time *The Visit*, so Matt went to this movie alone while waiting for his friend. He did not want to tell me about the twist in the movie in case I ever went to see it, but I assured him that I never would, so I got the Australian description of this horror film, with all of Matt's funny additives. I was still amazed that he sat through such a movie but realized that boredom can make you do crazy things. I teased him about this movie the whole time he spent with us, thus titling his chapter. I ended up having a great time with Mattie. Since Mattie was here, my daughter also decided to drive down and surprise us as well. Making memories is even more important to me now, and many more were made as we hung out, went to the beach, ate and ate and ate some more.

It takes a lot of eating to fill up seven feet of a man. His Australian humor and accent are so entertaining that I was thrilled having him around again. I knew when he left this time that I would not see him again until he or Shane got married, and neither of them are looking for that to happen anytime soon. So I bade him good-bye, wishing that he didn't live an ocean away but praising God for his life and the friendship he has had with my son. The visit was over, and everyone lived to tell about it, unlike the movie version.

<hr />

Even though I was constantly encouraged by internet friends and my family, I still found myself sad and disheartened some of the time. My boys, who were stuck with me all day, would reminded me, "My mother would never do this or that," forgetting that I will never be that person again, no matter how much physical healing occurs. It is depressing to realize that you have so many health problems you could pass at any time and miss out on so much. I know that we are commanded to look forward to heaven and our heavenly bodies, and that takes on a whole new meaning to me now. But it is difficult to live in the here and now knowing how dependent I am on others every day for the simplest things. My sons hate for me to cry, but at times I just bust loose and cannot control it. My tears always come from the pain that I know I cause others, who have to wait on me, cook for me, clean for me, and pay for me to live. And I don't know that it will ever go away. My dad will not allow me to cry either, and Nan makes sure that I know how useless it is to do so.

People think I am strong. But to tell the truth, I just want someone to hold me and let me cry while they genuinely tried to understand. That will never happen in this family, and somehow, that is all my fault. I have always disliked the cliché statements, but "Get over it," and "It's not about you" were two life statements that I tried to live by. God revealed these to me because I needed to accept them, but now they have defined me, allowing me no sympathy. Be very careful what you allow to define you. Make it about righteousness and holiness.

I look forward to many welcomed happy tears in the future as I master a prosthetic leg and begin to go when and where I want to go. I don't think that any of my loved ones will care if I tear up because I'm proud and happy that I am able to overcome a disability and move forward, literally. I long for this day with hope and even joy because of the days that I fell victim to believing that it may never come. I know that while I wait this day, I have to get involved in some type of volunteer work where I can be around people living life so that I can contribute in some way and glean some of their excitement for my own. I have to get back to where I can drive again so I can have the independence to go and do what I need to do, no matter what that takes.

Shane put my leg on and worked with me almost every day, but I never felt confident that this leg was the one I should have. I was constantly reminded of how easy it looked for all of those on TV, throwing the leg on and getting it done. The Pistorius trial was big in the news when I had my leg amputated, and the image of him replayed in my head often. I wanted to have one that I could just put on by myself, but having only one hand prevented it completely. My new prosthetist re-casted me, and as I waited for my second leg, I dreamed all the time of walking. I could put it on but still had some trouble getting my stump down in there and getting up.

My dad's second-floor railing in his condo served as a crutch, on which I could get more confident shifting my weight, but it proved to be the difficult. I went to his house often to walk, but because it was on the other side of town I became frustrated at how difficult it was to get to practice. If we had money, I could afford to get a leg that would work, but in our position, I could not even afford to think about prosthetic rehabilitation. It was frustrating.

I was advised to just wait until I was eligible for Medicare, which was only two short months away. With Shane leaving soon, I knew that my time was fleeing, and I did not have anyone else that was comfortable with walking me. I wanted to have accomplished this before Shane left, but it was too late. So I did all I could on my own and prayed that by the time I saw him next, he would see improvement.

Days were long, but to tell the truth, the nights took forever and the pain in my head worsened that I couldn't lie down, much less sleep. It was strange pain, every point where my head touched the pillow would throb, and I couldn't get much rest. Pain is a strange thing. It amazes me where it can take me, anywhere from depression to fear, regret to bitterness, or restlessness to hope and faith.

Today as I read my devotional, I realized that it had been a long time since I have experienced His unfathomable peace, and that's because I am not trusting Him like I used to or thanking Him like I should. I know better, but it has been so difficult. I have not put forth the effort and have gotten overwhelmed by our circumstances when I know I have to trust that the Creator who knows every hair on my head also knows every bad thing that is happening.

I have to trust that He is so much bigger than it all. I have chosen the natural responses when the Holy Spirit enables me to choose the supernatural response to all pain. I know that the supernatural can lift me above my circumstances.

I am sorry for all of those that I have not responded to properly. I am praying diligently that I can allow the Holy Spirit to guide me that I might be a better example to everyone dealing with sickness and healing. To all who have supported me in prayer for so long, waiting for me to report another miracle, be patient. I have had to relearn how to abide in Him because I have been abiding in my issues, believing that I had to focus so deeply to take the next step. It is such a calculated risk because if I fall down, it is likely that I will hurt myself and make another trip to the hospital, much like the one I've already taken. I lost my abiding love.

I am always concentrating on abiding in Him, knowing that the goal is perseverance, allowing the result therefore to be my perfection or completion. James 1:1–4 are great encouraging verses for me. It helps me so much to understand that it is all about finishing what God has started in me. I have to concentrate beyond reason to take each step no matter how painful or uncomfortable that is. God wants me to finish, no matter what it looks like. The only way to the finish line is through Him, every step. He can help me to take the next one.

Romans 8:28 is a verse that has passed over my lips every day for the last two and a half years. It says, "God works all things for good for those who know the Lord and are called according to His purpose." I am one of those called, so knowing that God always keeps His promises, I have to walk in trust.

For the first time, I walked in to church today with my cane, without the wheelchair. It was so difficult I wanted to just fall down in order to rest my muscles several times. But Mike encouraged me to push through it, and as I collapsed in the chair, I was proud and grateful. Pride was not an emotion that I had experienced in a long while, and it felt so wonderful to be proud of something besides the unending faith of my children. I listened intently to the message, not wanting to even think about having to leave, knowing how much effort it took to finally reach my seat. However, when the service ended and the crowd had cleared, I attempted to rise and grab for Mike in order to head back to the car. That day, more than any other,

I was so thankful for handicap parking because I knew my car was right outside the door. A young man who always took time to welcome us was there to take hold of my right side and open the doors as we began the long-dreaded walk to the car. Thank God that on this particular Sunday, no one was parked in the first parking space, so I could clearly see the car and was able to assess the amount of effort it would take to arrive there.

It is frustrating for me and my family to see someone healthy hop out of a vehicle in a handicap parking space, knowing how difficult it is for me to even get out of the car. Thank you to all of you who are convicted when you're about to take that space but change your mind knowing that you are blessed to be entitled to legs to walk on. Walk on!

By now, with so much time behind me, I should be able to write that I had a handle on all of this and was able to be happy in my circumstance. I still struggle every day, and my boys still remind me often that they are just glad I'm still here, no matter what else is going on. I don't think we can even know, in our flesh, what it means to surrender our all to Him. We can sing about it and even want it, but as much as I try to totally give up my every thought to Him, it is nearly impossible because we always have the option of taking it all back depending on our own strength again, which I usually do.

I still find myself wanting my husband or son to hug me and pat me on the back and not get frustrated with me when I have to ask to be taken to the restroom again and again. I say the words "I'm sorry" so many times a day to many people. It makes me a sorrowful person instead of the joyous person I was created to be. I know how it ruins my testimony of faith when I cry, but it is so tough to always be tough, and it tires me out as I struggle that it is the only expectation I am ever allowed. So it continues to haunt me and may until He takes me home or heals my life, whichever He chooses.

Living in the sunshine and thinking about how God allowed His son to shine in His suffering should be enough motivation for all of us to live every day that we are given to the very fullest, always making it difficult—no, impossible for those who know us to get into hell. I am deciding to smile in the face of adversity and command Satan to get behind me where he belongs, the only place that he is entitled to in my life because I belong to the one true King.

I cry often while talking to my mom on the phone because she is so far away, and I feel how hard it is for her not to be with me. My oldest son points out again how stupid it is for me to cry. I tried to explain to him that I have so many uncertainties, but he says, "That's life. Get over it." Much deserved advice.

He went on to tell me that I needed to just accept that I will possibly never walk again or just cry about it every day until I die. I disliked hearing that but love the simplicity of it all. I hope I can get beyond this, where it is not just a dream, but a reality. I am praying that my new defibrillator and attitude will help me feel less fatigue and give me more energy so that I might continue to endure and persevere.

I want to be an encouragement to anyone suffering from a stroke by saying that rehabilitation is possible, tears and confusion are to be expected, and God is so able. Keep courage and never quit. My expectation as a Christian is to make it hard for you to get into hell, so if you have never asked Jesus Christ to be your Savior, I can't even begin to tell you how to get through this. I could not have done it without Him. The Bible teaches that if you don't know Him, all you have to do is admit that you are a sinner in need of a Savior. Ask Him to come into your life and take up residency in your heart that you might be able to make better choices that would honor Him and not you. Then talk to Him about all of it, anything. He is always there. Read the Bible. Begin in John and learn to listen for Him to speak to you through His word. He always will, and all you have to do is apply what He says to your life, by trusting Him. The Bible encourages you to find a local church where you can establish the kind of friendships that have upheld me on my journey.

If you are a Christian, then He will be with you and guide you every step of the way, putting people in your life that you will need encouragement from to see you through. He will give you a way to endure every painful moment. All you have to do is love Him and thank Him more and more.

I have always believed that Eugene would work again, and now I see the importance of it even more, thinking that there would be so much more I could do on my own, plus how much it would help with my balance. I know how difficult it is for all of the people in my life, but at least they can walk away from it all when it gets to be too much. Mike goes to work, Shane can go play soccer or see a movie, but I can't ever get away from the fact of what a burden I am, much less walk away for a little quiet time for myself. I read my Bible and watch too much TV and continue to peck the computer keyboard trying to get *This Book* in order so that it might actually be published one day.

I am assured that *This Book* is a reason that all of this has happened to me and my family, and I know that I have not been the picture of faith that many have hoped I would be. But I am what He made me, and I am not giving up. It gets better and easier with each new day, and as I forgive myself more and more for not responding the way that Jonnie Erickison Tada did to her injuries, I am feeling more and more hopeful that God is going to repair the damage that my circumstances have caused my family, even if He does not repair me, so I pray about it daily. My dog, Kirby and I sit alone every day, and I have never been a loner, so I struggle some days with how to deal with it. Thank God I have *This Book*.

Since it takes two years after being deemed disabled before I am eligible for Medicare, I'm waiting for the day to come, thinking that it would be such a savings with future medical expenses only to realize that it only puts more rules and hoops to jump through in my life. Doesn't anyone know that one-legged people can't jump?

I could not get any in home health care due to the insurance carrier choice we made, even after much investigation, the company we chose would not grant me any help. In order to get someone to come in, I had to cancel my Medicare and re-enroll. After more waiting and hundreds of phone calls, I got a miracle named Claudia, an RN who visited me for one hour three times a week. She made many phone calls trying to get me on a Medicaid waiting list and counseled me on many health options. She would check my sugar and blood pressure on every visit. She would attend to my needs until my husband got home from work. There are many adult day-care facilities that would have been ideal for me, but you have to be sixty to be accepted; I am only fifty-seven. Just another hoop to jump around. Since my prosthetic is not exactly an extension of me as it should be, Claudia got me an appointment with a prosthetist in Tampa to evaluate me and assist with getting me one that will enable me to become more independent while I begin therapy.

I have now put all my prayers and hope in this new situation, believing this is the answer that the Lord has for me, praying that I will be enabled to serve Him again one day soon. I have many warriors uplifting me and believing this to be His plan. Patience has been redefined in my life as we await the next step on my journey. I am just thankful to be on it, wishing I had something wonderful to look forward to besides Christ's return.

I met another angel, Waldo Esparza in Tampa, and for the very first time, I looked into the eyes of someone I knew understood all that I was dealing with. He took my hand and prayed with me and then spoke to me honestly, knowing that it may not be exactly what I wanted to hear. He convinced me that I could truly do this, but I had to continue to work very hard to get it. He told me that my biggest problem was that I wanted to run in the Olympics without going through all of the state meets. I have to back up and accomplish the tough work of every match leading up to the big race. I went home from this appointment feeling good for the first time in a long time. I walked holding a railing, stepping through the pain, and hearing my sons' voices with each step telling me to look up or to follow through. That encouragement within my own head was very new to me, but I could master each new step because of it.

Performance excellence has always been important to me, and I never realized how much until now. I am ready to take the necessary steps backward in order to move forward, finally getting a better view of the big picture and being excited about it. I know now that I will someday walk alone, and I will press on until that day moving in whatever direction is necessary.

19

Black Sheep of the Family

Mike, my husband, was known as the black sheep of his family much because he did not attend the family college of choice but followed me to Murray State. I don't believe that many of them ever took him seriously as a Pastor, never coming to hear him preach. It was hard to even imagine how much God had changed him and I wanted so badly for his parents and family to see what I had seen. He pastored in a neighboring state that his grandmother also lived him, offering them an acceptable excuse to visit but it did not ever work out that way. I was very proud of the husband and the father he had become. I would have never thought that he would become the awesome public speaker and Pastor that he did. He was always shy and short, when we met in the eighth grade, but God took him to new heights for sure, and I got to go along with the ride. I always wished that there would come an opportunity for him to share where his family would be able to hear and enjoy him like we did.

Many grandparents, aunts and others passed away and married, but Mike was overlooked. Then Grandy, my step mother's mom, went to be with the Lord, and Missy asked Mike to say a few words at the graveside. I was so thankful and prayed that he would capture Grandy's immeasurable spirit in a miraculous way. He was great

KATHY MENDENHALL

because of God's grace and my family seemed pleased that he had contributed to the service. Family continued to get married and pass away without Mike being asked to help until his own mother died this year, and his father asked if he would say a few words in the service with Mee-Maw's church Pastor and her best friend. He struggled some when coming up with what approach to take but as he painted the picture of who his mother was, everyone responded in acceptance, and even some laughter, knowing that he captured her purpose beautifully. I was so proud and so thankful that he was allowed to be a part of such a wonderful service for an even more wonderful woman. God is so good and finally all of the family has heard the word of God from the son, brother, uncle, and dad that the Lord has built over these years. His plan is so perfect and I am thankful,

Since I spent 2 years looking at the world from a wheelchair most of those days, I have a new appreciation for all who are dependent on a chair or have disabilities that prevent them from communicating at eye level, it is very difficult. There have been many times that people would come and hold a door for my son as he drove me around but more times people have allowed doors to shut on us or snob us because I am lower and may not understand. It is so frustrating to not be able to see over the bottom shelves or being pushed so quickly I really can't see anything. I wanted to just push myself through Wal -mart and pick my own objects but only having one usable arm it is near impossible, so we do the best we can. Sitting beneath everyone's eye level made me feel less of a person and I so appreciated when someone would bend and speak to me on eye level. You feel like everyone is looking down on you, because they actually, physically are. Let me encourage everyone to take a minute to bend down and smile at someone in a chair and say hello, possibly encouraging them like I wished they had done for me. I will forever make that a part of my life when I walk again.

I was almost ashamed to attend church because I was always the type that would walk around and welcome everyone and if I felt the Spirit moving someone in the congregation I always wanted to accredit it and give them encouragement, now all I could do was sit and pray, not that prayer is not a valuable contribution, but I never felt like it was enough in these situations. The lack of personal inter-action makes you feel useless and alone. When I think back to how many times I have walked past someone in a wheelchair, for whatever reason, without offering them a smile or a good word I am ashamed and convicted simultaneously. There is no excuse why we don't take the time to encourage one another in this way, it takes little effort but offers everything in some circumstances. I love some of the hard lessons I have learned through this experience and I truly wouldn't change that. I am grateful and hope to start living as if I truly am. So many as they try to minister to me say, I can't ever understand what you've been through, but the important thing is the effort they make to understand and offer words of encouragement. Blessed am I because I have many friends that use God's word to encourage me as they tell me that they love and appreciate me. I am truly thankful for the friends that God has given me in life and especially in the 41 minutes of death because I know that without them and their prayers I would never have resumed breathing or have this opportunity to be an enduring overcomer.

I could never thank all of them, but God has used so many different ones to get me to where I am today, and I am not there yet, but so grateful. Today I am finally getting a defibulator put into my chest and connecting to my heart on Sept.11,2015. Since Mike and I were married on Sept 12, I spent another anniversary in a hospital bed, having hospital food for dinner and a sleepless night alone, until Shane got off work at 3AM and came by the hospital on his way home to check on me, since he had not seen me since my surgery. I was once again in that familiar pain, and then groggy from the mus-cle relaxer the nurse gave me. I only had to spend the night and could go home the next day so I was grateful that this was the first hospital that I wouldn't be there long enough to make good friends. The pain was so great the first night that I never went to sleep, but the follow-ing day I was able to sit up in the recliner and nap. I was still having a lot of pain on my stroke side and the Tylenol was not touching it or making me tired, but I knew I only had a week til the staples came out and then I would be able to talk to the Doctor more about why I was having the pain. The fifth night home I sat up again all night typing, hoping that I would get tired enough to sleep, but nothing. I had my feelings hurt often because my family did not understand that it was difficult for me to go to the restroom sometimes. I got so used to stressing out about planning when and how much to drink during those difficult times that it was still hard at times for me to go pee. My boys and husband would constantly tell me how stupid it was, "either you have to go or you don't", they would say, and I would get so upset that I couldn't make myself go, it would hurt me to hear them talk about it for what seemed like all of the time. Planning bathroom stops had become a way of life for me because I was unable to go alone and it would always fall on my son to take me. He was not going into a ladies restroom and was too embarrassed to take me to a men's so there always had to be a single stall bathroom everywhere I went. I always peed before I left the house but sometimes I had something to drink while we were out and couldn't help from having to go again. This had become a huge deal for me that I believe did some permanent damage. They still had me taking a small amount of Lasix saying that I needed it for the swelling around my heart. If I had a female caregiver I don't think it would have ever been an issue but with my situation it certainly was. I felt like I had to have the daily plan before I was ever comfortable leaving my home. The stress that this added to my life certainly wasn't healthy but I felt responsible since I didn't want to add to the inconvenience I already was to everyone's life. The hardest thing for all of us is completely surrendering ourselves to others, but is required when you are completely dependent for assistance to urinate, it is even hard to do with Jesus, whom we know is the author and finisher of our faith, and much harder to do to someone you deeply love without feeling guilt of the burden you are to them. I know that I don't even distinguish between feelings anymore. I'm not happy or sad, I'm just having feelings, both of which make me cry and then I get fussed at because without understanding, everyone in my life sees it as weakness or self-pity. This becomes dangerous mentality as well because it makes me want to shut everyone out just so I don't risk having feelings that may lead to tears then to fussing. I have the hardest time with my oldest son on this and we end up saying hurtful things to one another, making me wish I had never opened up in the first place saving us both the trouble. Our minds are intercut things and I have never been a psychology student, almost failing 101 in college and never agreeing with most of the philosophies since I believe many of them contradict scriptures. I don't need to go very deep when I think about all of this, just trust and move on, and if I had taken my own advice I may be farther along, who knows, probably the psychologists I've never seen?

Contentment is hard for me to find and I still feel sadness and like I am very much a disappointment to so many who love me, but "This Book" has helped me so much because it has given me something that is just mine, not depending on anyone else as I type along with one finger, praying that I can get to an ending that might bring some closure in my life as well. I am tossed into bed each evening by my husband and try to roll to my left side but it doesn't last long before my chest hurts so badly I have to try to roll the other way, leaving my arm behind causing great pain. I try to dig my arm out from under me and bend it so that it can rest across my waist, hanging off the right side of the bed. I can make this side last longer because my chest doesn't hurt as bad, but when Mikes phone blares "Amazing Grace", at five AM I am always ready to get up. I just struggle to lie down for a long period of time, resulting in me spending a lot of time in the recliner, where I struggle to write. I also find it very difficult to get into my wheelchair from the recliner because the chair is so low.

My oldest son, who has a little of me in him put a lot in perspective for me when on one of my sad days, told me that he knew that if this trauma had not happened in my life he would not be here with his family even though it was his favorite place to be. He said that he probably wouldn't be here with his dad or siblings if it weren't for this stroke and everything that followed. If that was the only reason this happened it would be enough because family is so very important and Jared had already missed out on so much, by choice, that I was extremely grateful that he was choosing us now. He would get up any time, day or night to take me to the bathroom or do whatever I needed. He never made me feel bad about asking him to do for me but always expressed that it was the least he could do. God has given me a beautiful family and I truly thank God for them all. Jared made my breakfast every morning, allowing his brother to sleep in, since he worked all night. He was so good to us and it was such a relief because he had abused these relationships for so long. I am so grateful that God enabled us to come together as a family again. Jared continued to try to make me laugh as he would lay with me on the floor as I sat in the recliner. He kept me from ever feeling lonely and allowed me to get back to counting my blessings. **(thanks Jared)**. I think that the toughest part of this now is having no privacy at all, someone has to accompany me to everything I do, so it is difficult feeling like I do not have any time to myself. I went to outpatient therapy at the request of my neurologist and he injected my arm with another dosage of Botox. After several weekly visits of therapy for my arm. My PT told me there was no use in me coming back therefore if my arm comes back at all it will be because of the work I am doing on my own. He gave me a pretty good massage but that was it. They never instructed me on how to connect and try to voluntarily move Eugene. I try to work it out every night for an hour, but it usually makes me so sad to see how weak I have become and how little movement my left side knows. Day after day I have to continue to give it all the hope I can muster up and pray that God will enable it to remember how to function. Knowing that at any time my arm could awaken and function normally again. "Hope is still in front of me." I would sing it if I could only carry a tune.

CPSIA information can be obtained
at www.ICGtesting.com
Printed in the USA
LVHW072146100119
603541LV00017B/162/P